CUMM'
32
WILM

TELEP   508   2016   7/22/88

Dear Stewardess:

I wanted to get this book to you before I left the plane but it didn't work out.

I want you to know that I enjoyed talking with you and hope to see you again.

With Cummings

DR. RICHARD D. CUMMINGS

Dear Davy & Jason of Found Magazine,

Hi guys! I love the magazine so much. I have been collecting found letters since I was about twelve in Maine with my puritanical grandfather. We were walking along the coast, trying to figure out how to relate to each other, when we came across the torn and tear stained remnants of a love letter/break-up note. It was torn into about fifteen pieces and contained some raunchy and heartfelt nuggets. My grandfather started laughing – very unexpected – and read the contents out loud as he found them. By the end of our walk we actually liked each other. Yes, brought together by the found scribblings of a stranger.

Now, 20 years later, I have a large collection of found items (although, for some reason not the original artifact) which I treasure almost above all else. So, Found Magazine was a revelation -- I was so happy when I realized I wasn't alone in my obsession with other people's written business.

Thanks!

Lizzy

Lizzy Waronker

I'll send one of my favorite found pieces...... "Dear Stewardess" for your enjoyment. Sort of as payback for all the enjoyment Found Mag has given me.

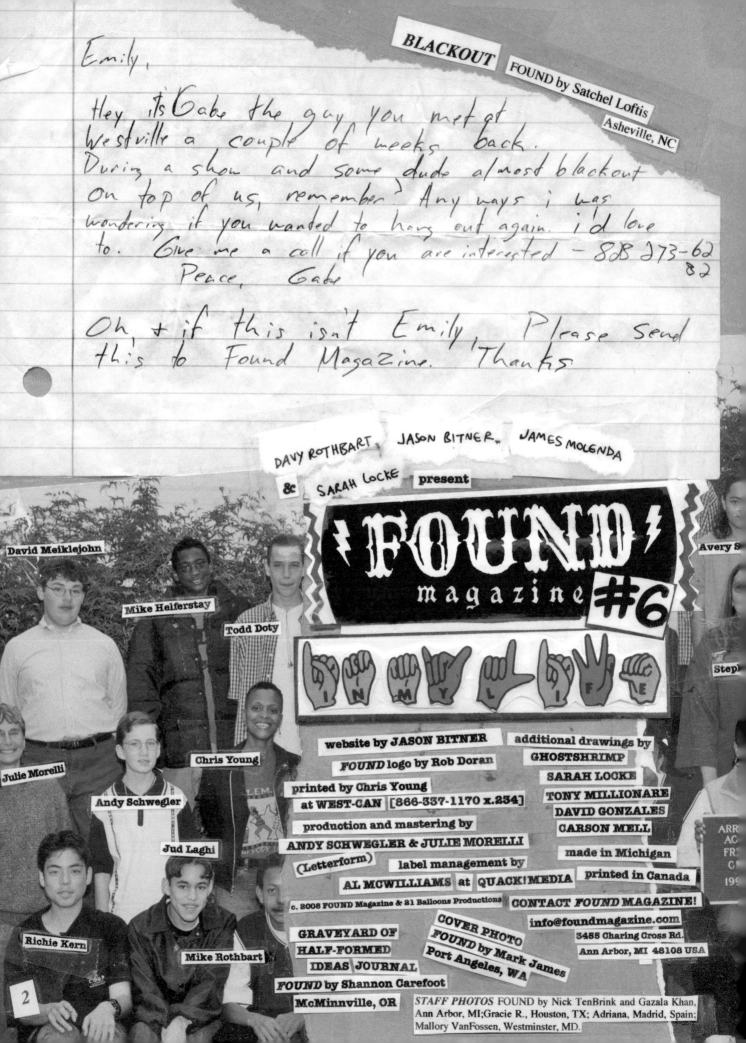

Emily,

Hey, it's Gabe the guy you met at
Westville a couple of weeks back.
During a show and some dude almost blackout
on top of us, remember? Any ways i was
wondering if you wanted to hang out again. i'd love
to. Give me a call if you are interested – 808 273-62
          Peace, Gabe   82

Oh, & if this isn't Emily, Please Send
this to Found Magazine. Thanks

BLACKOUT FOUND by Satchel Loftis
Asheville, NC

DAVY ROTHBART, JASON BITNER, JAMES MOLENDA
& SARAH LOCKE present

FOUND
magazine #6

[IN MY LIFE — sign language hands]

David Meiklejohn
Mike Helferstay
Todd Doty
Avery S
Steph
Julie Morelli
Chris Young
Andy Schwegler
Jud Laghi
Richie Kern
Mike Rothbart

website by **JASON BITNER**
FOUND logo by Rob Doran

printed by Chris Young
at WEST-CAN [866-337-1170 x.234]
production and mastering by
ANDY SCHWEGLER & JULIE MORELLI
(Letterform) label management by
AL MCWILLIAMS at **QUACK! MEDIA**
c. 2008 FOUND Magazine & 21 Balloons Productions

GRAVEYARD OF
HALF-FORMED
IDEAS JOURNAL
FOUND by Shannon Carefoot
McMinnville, OR

COVER PHOTO
FOUND by Mark James
Port Angeles, WA

additional drawings by
GHOSTSHRIMP
SARAH LOCKE
TONY MILLIONARE
DAVID GONZALES
CARSON MELL

made in Michigan
printed in Canada

CONTACT *FOUND* MAGAZINE!
info@foundmagazine.com
3455 Charing Cross Rd.
Ann Arbor, MI 48108 USA

STAFF PHOTOS FOUND by Nick TenBrink and Gazala Khan,
Ann Arbor, MI; Gracie R., Houston, TX; Adriana, Madrid, Spain;
Mallory VanFossen, Westminster, MD.

2

FOUND magazine #6

STAFF!

JAMES MOLENDA

PETER ROTHBART

DAVY ROTHBART
point guard

JASON BITNER
power forward

SARAH LOCKE

Kimberly Chou

Amanda Patten

Amanda Bullock

BRANDE WIX

Lauren Spiegel

Andrew Cohn

Mike DiBella

Brett Loudermilk

Javan Makhmali

Arthur Jones

Al McWilliams

Barbara Brodsky

Michelle Quint

Hal "Big Poppa" Rothbart

DREAMS REALLY DO COME TRUE

FOUND by Vera Bruptly
San Francisco, CA

I my god!
I so want to
be in the
found note
magazine!

3

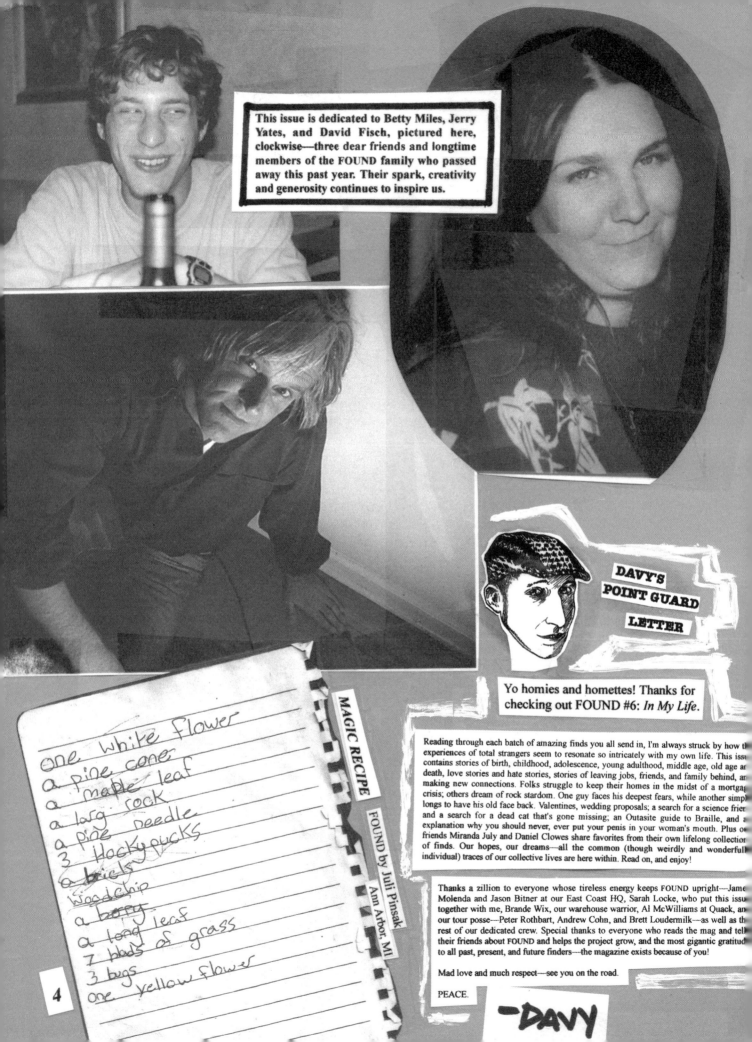

This issue is dedicated to Betty Miles, Jerry Yates, and David Fisch, pictured here, clockwise—three dear friends and longtime members of the FOUND family who passed away this past year. Their spark, creativity and generosity continues to inspire us.

MAGIC RECIPE

FOUND by Juli Pinsak
Ann Arbor, MI

one white flower
a pine cone
a maple leaf
a larg rock
a pine needle
3 Hockypucks
a brick
woodchip
a berry
a long leaf
7 blads of grass
3 bugs
one yellow flower

DAVY'S POINT GUARD LETTER

Yo homies and homettes! Thanks for checking out FOUND #6: *In My Life*.

Reading through each batch of amazing finds you all send in, I'm always struck by how the experiences of total strangers seem to resonate so intricately with my own life. This issue contains stories of birth, childhood, adolescence, young adulthood, middle age, old age and death, love stories and hate stories, stories of leaving jobs, friends, and family behind, and making new connections. Folks struggle to keep their homes in the midst of a mortgage crisis; others dream of rock stardom. One guy faces his deepest fears, while another simply longs to have his old face back. Valentines, wedding proposals; a search for a science friend and a search for a dead cat that's gone missing; an Outasite guide to Braille, and an explanation why you should never, ever put your penis in your woman's mouth. Plus our friends Miranda July and Daniel Clowes share favorites from their own lifelong collections of finds. Our hopes, our dreams—all the common (though weirdly and wonderfully individual) traces of our collective lives are here within. Read on, and enjoy!

Thanks a zillion to everyone whose tireless energy keeps FOUND upright—James Molenda and Jason Bitner at our East Coast HQ, Sarah Locke, who put this issue together with me, Brande Wix, our warehouse warrior, Al McWilliams at Quack, and our tour posse—Peter Rothbart, Andrew Cohn, and Brett Loudermilk—as well as the rest of our dedicated crew. Special thanks to everyone who reads the mag and tells their friends about FOUND and helps the project grow, and the most gigantic gratitude to all past, present, and future finders—the magazine exists because of you!

Mad love and much respect—see you on the road.

PEACE.

-DAVY

4

10/24

To my friends at FOUND:

I found this mail waiting to be picked up by you.

As you can see, it has been waiting a while, so I put some extra postage on it so it could continue on its way.

PEACE!

Your friendly neighborhood Postal clerk ......

Thanks Anita and Chad and all our friends at the Ann Arbor post office!

LOWER YOUR PRICES
FOUND by Ben Meiklejohn

Acton, ME

Orchard School
Baldwin Avenue
50 th Burlington V.t. 054
February 4, 1986

Dear Ice cream man,
How are you doing? How many ice cream cones have you sold? I wanted to remind you to stop by my house and lower your prices.
Only give me Bubble gum ice cream.

Your friend,
David

CANNOT WAIT
FOUND by Laurie Murphy

Watertown, MA

Dear NBA Wrappers Rebound Redemption people,

I have enclosed UPC codes from 40 various NBA products wrappers. I am sorry but I mailed UPC codes cause with my allowance I can not affort to mail a package full of empty wrappers which costs $3.60 to $4.95. I already have spent my money on the cards and I had to ask my brother to write me a cheque for shipping and handling.

I hope that you will understand me and process my request cause I can hot wait to get a SHAQ EXCLUSIVE set for my basketball collection.

Thank you in-advance.

Ivan Dragelj

1037- 6TH AVENUE
NEW WESTMINSTER , B.C.
V3M 2B7
CANADA   (604)443-0065

CUSTOMER SERVICE
FOUND by Tim McAllister

Grand Rapids, MI

December 23, 1998

Celestial Seasonings, Inc.
5505 36th Street SE
Grand Rapids, MI 49512
(800) 2000-TEA

Miss Catherine Brazell
17800 Jordan Road
Arlington, WA 98223

Miss Brazell,

We apologize for you not receiving your Nutcracker Embossed Holiday Tin. We understand how much you were looking forward to getting it. We hope you had a merry Christmas, and will have a happy New Year, you little nazi bitch.

Customer Service
Celestial Seasonings

I hope I'm ~~this~~ ~~kids of america~~ kid helping you to be able to play. you guys relly need this. I'm Dakota from Iowa. oh and here. have fun. your welcome too Dye.

ATTENTION BOOKSELLERS

Important Announcement

The title stenciled on this carton is fictitious and was used for security reasons.

The books in the carton — *I Want to Tell You* by O. J. Simpson — are what you ordered.

Please put them on sale immediately.

Thanks.

DEAR KIDS OF AMERICA

FOUND by Erin Tapken
Marion, IA

I was working at the Salvation Army's Toys for Tots distribution center, and found this delightful nugget rolled up and tucked under the arm of a little bear that had been donated.

—E.T.

I WANT TO TELL YOU

FOUND by Holly Smith
Birmingham, MI

PEANUT BUTTER POPCORN

FOUND by Francesca Stulano
Stillwater, MN

I found this picture clipped to this note in an old desk.　—F.S.

Please have Caleb take re-takes. Try to get him to smile by teasing him or saying silly things like "peanut butter popcorn", "You're a big dill pickle", etc. Thanks,

Is Caleb's notebook at school!?

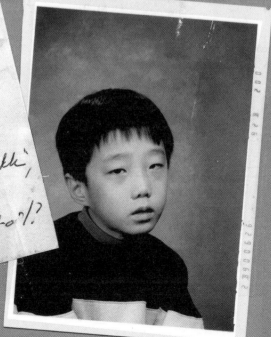

6

I WANT MY FACE BACK

FOUND by Ben Carpenter

San Francisco, CA

this drawing FOUND by Heinz Lotz, Darmstadt, Germany

I WANT MY ~~D~~ FACE BACK, Dr. DOICHI.
DO YOU HEAR ME? YOO TOOK IT AWAY FROM ME AND
I WANT IT BACK ~~NOW~~. I KNOW I PAID YOU FOR IT ~~ALL~~.
~~A WAIT BACK NOW~~. I DON'T CARE ABOUT MONEY.
IT'S NOT THE MONEY. IT'S JUST I WANT MY OLD FACE BACK.
   PUT THE PHONE DOWN. YOUR SECREATRY IS TIED UP - LITERALLY.
I KOW GUNS. I SPENT THE LAST SIX WEEKS
LEARNING GUNS — EVER SINCE I CALLED
AND YOUR SECRETARY TOLD ME YOU WERE BOOKED UP
FOR MONTHS. I CAN'T'S WAIT FOR MONTHS,
I WANT MY OLD FACE BACK RIGHT NOW.
   YOU TOLD ME I'D HAVE A ~~NEW~~ WHOLE NEW LEASE ON LIFE
WHAT DOES THAT MEAN DR. DOICHI? I WANTED ~~A~~ NEW LOOK
NOT NEW PEERS. I LIKED MY PEERS. I MISS
MY WONDERFUL OLD FRIENDS'. THEY CAN'T STAND TO LOOK AT ME NOW
BECAUSE IT MAKES THEM FEEL OLD. I FEEL
JUST LIKE THEM AND I DON'T FIT IN ANYMORE, Dr DOICHI.

FOUND Magazine. You guys relly need this.

7

MAD OR SAD

FOUND by Andrew Cohn

Los Angeles, CA

I think it's cause i grind and you don't trim. so it irritates me. It all makes sense :) Don't be mad or sad

PROBLEMS   FOUND by Ruby Wendell   Iowa City, IA

EVERYBODY HAS PROBLEMS — BUT THE THING IS NOT TO MAKE A PROBLEM ABOUT YOUR PROBLEMS —

front

back

Mom —

~~Envelopes~~ Envelopes (manilla) are in drawer marked ~~"manilla envelopes"~~ "Manilla Envelopes" on right

— Meredith ♥

CONFUSION→
6/03

→ CHAOS → CATASTROPHE
1/05   ↓
         COLLAPSE

JO

THE THRILLA IN MANILLA

FOUND by Satchel Loftis

Richmond, VA

TOUGH ROAD

FOUND by Nora Sweeney   Redwood City, CA

I found this on the floor at Main Street Coffee Roasting Company. My question is: When did Catastrophe and Collapse occur?
—N.S.

Fredrick Douglass
My Bong

SELF-REALIZATION

FOUND by Paul

San Luis Obispo, CA

HANDYMAN CLUB OF AMERICA MEMBER

Mary : Brandy:
1/2 Milk, & Thinking
Of You Card

THINKING OF YOU

FOUND by Allison Libby

South Portland, ME

Self-Realization
Fellowship Temples & Retreats

SCHEDULE OF SERVICES

You have stated that you are "frank" but yet you are not telling me your unsatisfaction about your happiness and progress or lack of progress. Using that as an exc. for masterbation.

JULY · AUGUST · SEPTEMBER

The man I fell in love 2006 w. was innocent, not aware of and selfabsorbed. Did not bug excessively. Was sexual but not perverse. Would never fuck a 22yr "slut"

*"Giving love to all, feeling the love of God,
seeing His presence in everyone…
that is the way to live in this world."*
— Paramahansa Yogananda

Self-Realization Fellowship
FOUNDED 1920
Paramahansa Yogananda

9

MADE RIGHT

FOUND by John Lunardini

Jackson, MS

John and his co-workers found a wallet in an empty lo[...]
belonging to a guy named Ricky Saunders. All attempts t[...]
find him and return his wallet failed. Inside was this not[...]
from Ricky's fiancée—I wonder how things turned out?
The wallet contained conflicting clues—a receipt for [...]
dutiful jewelry-store payments, presumably for the ring,
but also another girl's phone number on a scrap of paper.

—DAVY

DEPOSIT GUARANTY MORTGAGE COMPANY
Jackson, Mississippi

Correspondent Lending
Phone: 1-800-748-3000, ext. 6829
Fax: 601-960-6047

Hi Ricky,

I'm at work thinking about you and our future together. These last 2 days have been confusing. I have questions that only God have the answer to. I must be patient and wait for my answers to be revealed to me. One of my questions is: What should our living arrangement be between now and our wedding day? Should you stay with me or your father?

DEPOSIT GUARANTY MORTGAGE COMPANY
Jackson, Mississippi
2

Correspondent Lending
Phone: 1-800-748-3000, ext. 6829
Fax: 601-960-6047

Although it was great to wake up to you this morning, I believe it will be better for us if you stay with your father. (I'll explain this in person) You were right, this relationship will not progress until I make more effort to believe you when you say you will not hurt me again. My defenses are up so high because I can't stop imagining you with Casandra. All the time I was thinking you were faithful to me was just a lie. When people asked me was I sure about settling

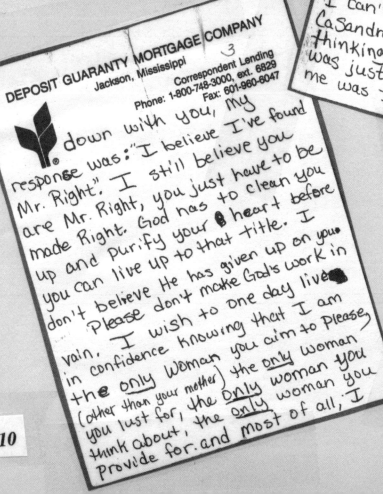

DEPOSIT GUARANTY MORTGAGE COMPANY
Jackson, Mississippi
3

Correspondent Lending
Phone: 1-800-748-3000, ext. 6829
Fax: 601-960-6047

down with you, my response was: "I believe I've found Mr. Right". I still believe you are Mr. Right, you just have to be made Right. God has to clean you up and purify your heart before you can live up to that title. I don't believe He has given up on you. Please don't make God's work in vain. I wish to one day live in confidence knowing that I am the only woman you aim to please, (other than your mother) the only woman you lust for, the only woman you think about, the only woman you provide for. and most of all, I

FOUND by Geoff Wright, Windham, ME

10

DEPOSIT GUARANTY MORTGAGE COMPANY
Jackson, Mississippi

4

Correspondent Lending
Phone: 1-800-748-3000, ext. 6829
Fax: 601-960-6047

want 🖤 you. to love me so much that you wont have room to love anyone else. This is how I feel about you.

As we Pray and work together to make this relationship/Marriage work, we must Remember to keep God first and In all our getting, we must acknowledge Him.

You went to God asking to be forgiven and you promised to never hurt me, again. He heard you and forgives you, therefore I forgive you also. But, our test is not over

DEPOSIT GUARANTY MORTGAGE COMPANY
Jackson, Mississippi

5

Correspondent Lending
Phone: 1-800-748-3000, ext. 6829
Fax: 601-960-6047

yet. It has just Started you must Prove to God that your prayer request is sincere and you will do what ever it takes to make Him believe you. I look forward to meeting the NEW Ricky Saunders.

We are a couple put 🖤 together by God and what God 🖤 has created, let NO man destroy.

I truly love you.
Keisha
5/12/2000

```
MARKS & MORGAN
JEWELERS SINCE 1909
STORE # 0142

METROCENTER MALL
1306, METROCENTER SPACE 56
JACKSON, MS 39209

BEN- 1        11/02/99        0142
0001/02/003646    PAYMENTS
                            50.00
                            50.00
PAYMENT 6011800200683149      .00
CASH
CHANGE DUE

61MARKS & MORGAN JEWELERS METROCENTER
TRUST US TO MAKE IT SPECIAL WITH
DIAMONDS, GEMSTONES, GOLD & MORE
```

BLACK OPAL®
Advanced Treatment for Black Skin

NOTES

Jenica
292-6679

BLACK
OPA

Dear You,
Theres good news and bad news. The good news is
that the cake turned out quite alright, well
maybe 60-70% decent so I didnt disgrace myself.
The bad news is that ~~the rest of~~ our New
South Wales tour has been cancelled because
Nicholas wants to go to a wedding that weekend,
a fucking wedding!! When he first informed
the band of the situation it didnt affect me
so much but the whole thing has been playing
on my mind all week. Man, this was such
a good gig we had lined up, and all over a
fucking wedding. When you play in a band
so much of your life, your future, your
rock 'n' roll dreams are tied up in the
whims and decisions of others, and sometimes
~~when you are walking along Nicholson~~
street during a break from pumping out
life-changing jams in the rehearsal room
so you can eat a falafel your legs start
to all move in synch together and you
walk along Nicholson Street like you are
The Ramones walking along Nicholson Street
or Sonic Youth walking along...... some busy
street in New York City where all that
steam comes out of the drains or maybe
you walk along the street like you play
lead guitar in Van Halen and its
1986 and the street is Sunset Strip, or
you walk along the street and realise
that you're in The Ramones, and you hate
~~the rest of~~ the rest of the band or you are
Thurston Moore and have just had all

of your ~~guitars~~ specially customed guitars stolen by junkie morons, or you are Van Halen and realise that its no longer 1986 or you're Joy Division or Nirvana and you've just found out that your band is now one member smaller. I hate weddings. I've only been to two in my life. The first was when my Aunty Gill got married to Dave when I was about six years old and all I remember is fighting with all of the other kids at the after wedding party. The second wedding was at my not so ~~close~~ friends ~~Effie~~ and Alex which kind felt like the experience of flushing my life-savings down a toilet, and not in a good way. Usually I'm on the same page with my band, we are a band, we stand together strong like like like like like ..... a rock and roll band! Yes!!! And now this wedding has made me feel like ~~one of~~ a drunk in a Gillian wearing video. But im going to get over it, im going to move on, let my negative thoughts go so we can walk to the falafel shop and eat the falafel then get back in the rehearsal ~~s~~ room and kick out the ~~jams~~ jams mother fucker!!!

I'll speak to you ~~of~~ again soon.

from Luke.

Over a million U.S. homeowners have lost their homes due to foreclosures since the mortgage crisis began in the summer of 2007. In a Dumpster behind an office building, Rick found this stack of faxes from people requesting loans and help with financing (or re-financing) their mortgages. These plaintive appeals for help offer an intricate look into the sour twists of fate that can leave hard-working, well-meaning people with their backs against the wall.

—DAVY

To whom it may concern:

My name is Josephine B. Webber and I am the property owner of 188 Griffin Avenue, Riverside, California.

I am writing this letter in explanation for my financial difficulties which resulted in my home being placed in foreclosure on 2 occasions and my filing Chapter 13 on 3 occasions. The reasons for the foreclosures and Chapter 13 filings are as follows:

I have, for the past 13 years been employed as a paralegal. I began to experience financial difficulties when I re-married approximately 9 years ago. My then new husband owed a sizable amount of child support arrearage. The local District Attorney Office would, without warning, seize nearly the entire amount of my spouse's paycheck, leaving our family just a few hundred dollars, when his paycheck for the week was customarily nearly $1,500.00 due to his pay scale of $36.00 per hour. Our family depended heavily on my husband's paycheck for payment of my mortgage and insurances. My paycheck, on the other hand, paid for monthly utilities in addition to food, clothing and childcare. During these times I would build up a reserve of money, only to have it depleted when my husband's wages were garnished.

Further, approximately 3 ½ years ago my husband and 2 year old daughter were involved in nearly fatal auto accident when a drunk driver broadsided our vehicle on a major highway in Rancho Cucamonga, CA. They were trapped in the vehicle and had to be extracted from our vehicle using the famed "Jaws of Life" machine. Due to the severe nature of both their injuries, each was airlifted to a local trauma center where my husband's left arm was re-attached and our little girl's wounds and lacerations to her tiny face were mended.

In conclusion, nearly 2 years ago my husband left our family and I have taken on additional employment to cover my family's expenses. My teenage daughter, Genesis, is a high school student and works a part-time job tutoring elementary school student in order to offset her expenses and assist our family toward financial recovery.

Sincerely,

Josephine B. Webber

Josephine B. Webber

14

Rev. Richard Johnson
3455 Fernwood St.
Oakland, IL 60453

To Whom It May Concern:

The following information is provided to address issues and items found in my credit report pulled in support of my request to obtain a first mortgage on my residence at 3455 Fernwood Street, Oakland, IL 60453.

Regarding the allegation that I am in arrears on child support. Many years ago I did have a relationship with the mother of the child. However, I have steadfastly maintained that I am NOT the father of the child in question. Furthermore, NO court has declared me to be the child's father. Additionally NO tests have ever been conducted which showed that I am the father of the child.

Regarding the numerous delinquent accounts that appear on my credit report. These debts were incurred during the very early years of my ministry when I was devoting all of my time, effort, energy and personal resources into establishing my church. Unfortunately, I regret to say that I lost focus of my financial obligations and this resulted in my becoming financially over extended. Currently, my church has grown and prospered. I am diligently striving to get my financial house in order and will conduct my future business dealings in a more responsible manner.

Sincerely,

Richard Johnson

Rev. Richard Johnson

To Whom it May Concern:

I, James L. Clark, am writing this letter to explain my current Credit situation. I was married last year to my current wife, Sandra. At the time of my marriage my wife was a Manager at at a local Hotel. Shortly after our marriage my wife had several heart attacks, after that we discovered that my wife had problems with her Diabetes due to the fact that she has Rheumatoid Arthritis, Fibramalagia, Lupus and Neuropothy caused from the Diabetes. My wife then suffered a stroke last November and we found out that she has Bone Cancer which is being currently treated with Chemotherapy. My wife applied for Social Security Benefits and was recently denied (which we were told from the very beginning that all are denied the first time), we have hired an Attorney and the case goes to Court next year. We have been assured that we will recieve back pay retroactive to the last day that she worked. Then this year I was in an accident that left me impaired and unable to work for a short while, I have been back to work for sometime. In May of this year I went to my local bank to withdraw money and found that my account had a negative balance. After further investigation by the Branch Manager we found several Debit transactions that I did not authorize. Someone had obtained my card number and made several on-line transactions. The perpetrator has been caught (a local 17 year old that worked

continues on the next page →

← continued from the previous page

at a Steak house here in town that waited on me at the restaraunt and copied my Debit card numbers when he ran my card) and arrested, we are currently waiting to go to trial. This young man also opened Credit Cards in my name and recently charged up several Credit Cards to their maximum limits. I was a victim of Identity Theft. Upon applying for this loan, the loan officer gave me my Credit Report and go over the charges and let me know which ones were mine and the ones that were the ones dealing with Identity theft. Looking at the accounts I noticed that several of the accounts were ones that my late deceased wife had during our Marriage. I then contacted my ex mother-in-law and told her since she is executor of the Estate she needed to pay for these balances since the Will stated all debts in her name would be paid for. She has refused to pay for these and since I am her husband I am legally bound to these. I hired an Attorney and we are hoping to settle these accounts out of Court, but we are prepared to take Legal action if necessary. All of the other Debts besides the three with First Tennesse that I am currently asking for this loan are currently be taking care of through a debt consolodation company. Then all of the Identity theft ones and the ones through my ex-wife Susan's estate will be taken care of at a later date.

I am a hard working man who currently has had some problems. I am taking care of these to the best of my abilities.

Sincerely yours,

James L. Clark

James L. Clark

02/15/2007

To whom it may concern, this is to inform you that due to a loss of two babies, we have been experiencing hardship during 2005-2006.

We have since then regain our composer and are on the way to a much better future. My husband has had three wage increases since then and has been moved to a higher position.

I own my own business and I am now back to work and fully intend on repairing my credit and improving on my standers of living.

Thank You,

Stan and Leewina Rodriguez

Stan Rodriguez

Leewina Rodriguez

What would this loan do for me? First it would stop my place of

living, from being repossessed. The second reason is to clean up ... to fix or replace items

First let me explain myself. I'am a 39 year old Male, with a loven and supportive Wife. I Have 3 kids. My kid Have been diagonse with Autism of Various Degrees.

To: kc@ablemortgage.net

Subject: Curry - Countrywide Mortgage

Our mortgage was sold to Countrywide approx. 1 1/2 years ago. We had our house on the market February 2004, and we had an offer the first day. Unfortunately, we knew the young couple and they kept putting us off and getting extensions. We used 2 months of our mortgage money to make repairs to our home the couple said was needed to get their insurance and we put money down on a new home for us. In the end of July, the week of the closing, the couple said they could not get a mortgage! Our lawyer had just called Countrywide for a payoff so they were aware of what was going on. When this happened I called Countrywide immediately to make arrangements to catch up on the 2 months we were behind. 2 days later a sheriff was at our door with foreclosure papers. We had to borrow money from Dennis' mother's estate (which we are entitled to on a yearly basis) but the catch was that our brother-in-law is the one that handles this. Countrywide would only work with him exclusively, even though it is our mortgage. He sent them a check from the estate to get the house out of foreclosure. 1 month later they returned the check, to us, not him, saying they would only accept a certain way of payment and we now had more money owed for finance charges, late charges, etc. Our brother-in-law sent them the acceptable form of payment. It is now September and we still have not heard from Countrywide. Our brother-in-law has not heard anything, nor has our attorney. I finally called them the beginning of October and forced them to talk to me and they replied "You're out of foreclosure but it's not our responsibility to notify you". We received no correspondence, either letter, monthly bill, nothing! They told us you are already 1 month behind! I made a payment in October, November, and in December I had to skip a payment as we had everything happen at once. Furnace went, 2 tires on our car blew, etc. Made a payment in January, in February I was short $200 but I sent the rest of the payment ($1434.00). I sent a payment in March and April. April 30th I received the bank check back (I made all my payments with a bank check) with a letter dated 4/21 (attached). I called to ask them why they sent the payment back and they told me I was 4 months behind. I asked them how that could be and their way of thinking was the 1 payment behind I started with, December, February and April. I explained I sent a payment in February that was just $200 short and they said they applied that to principal and late charges, not as a payment. I asked them why they did that instead of letting me know, or returning it. They explained that was what they had decided to do. Just as we were getting to the reason they returned the April payment, guess what, a sheriff knocked on my door with foreclosure papers! I went ballistic. I made arrangements immediately for a work-out program. I am now paying $2300 per month for 12 months. I have paid that 4 months already. Countrywide does not communicate and when you try to call them it is almost impossible to speak to a "live" person instead of a recording, and then you can never get the same person twice. No extensions. We have paid on a monthly basis for the mortgage. When an emergency arises, it is impossible to talk with them and work anything out. Anything you can do to get us a different mortgage would be appreciated. If you need more information, please let me know.

Thank you,
Dennis & Susan Anderson

As part of my exit strategy after 6 to 9 months to get a refinance to lower the interest rate on the loan. This refinance will be done with Trump Capital help. In the mean time I'am actively looking for a full time job. While I'am looking I will work for Wal-mart on a full time bases. To sum up, this load will place me in a better position to help my family in the long term of life. If any doubted about making payment of this loan, just look at my work history. 12 plus years working two jobs, 1 full time and 1 part time. I will continue to work two jobs to get this loan paid off. I thank all for there time and effort in getting me ...

How I got in to debit.

Borrower Call: Howard and Nanette Mosser 407-230-7240

The borrower's purchased the property for 171K in September of 2001. At the time, they put down about 15K. Since the date of purchase, the borrowers have done some landscaping, but other than that, no significant improvements have been made.

Mr. Mosser currently works for Walt Disney World as a music director. He has been with the company for over 15 yrs. He makes a bare minimum of $25 per hour, but can make more. Since it is an entertainment business, each venue, etc has a different pay scale. But again, minimum amount per hour is $25 and he works a minimum of 40 hrs per week (most of the time more).

Mrs. Mosser currently works for Florida Hospital. She started there in February of 2005. She is making approximately $12 per hour, but just received a promotion that will take place in the next month or so. Prior to this job, she was also working with Walt Disney World. She was there for 13 yrs, but left due to pay structure.

The Mosser's credit issues began back in 2001, shortly after Sept. 11th and have snowballed since then. Since they are both in the entertainment business, the business they were in took a significant hit. They actually moved into this home on the 14th (the walk through was on the 11th). As a result of Sept. 11th **Mrs. Mosser** did not work for 3 months. She was a dancer, etc at the time. Thus, their savings was drained. Over the last few yrs, they have been living paycheck to paycheck and are just looking for a breather at this point. Also, the borrowers have a son that is 8 yrs old and one that is 2.5. Prior to the 2 yr old, **Mrs. Mosser** was on fertility drugs. She had stopped a few months before getting pregnant as they continued to have trouble actually getting pregnant. A few months later (15wks pregnant), she actually found out she was pregnant. At 19 wks she was put on bed rest due to complications. Her son was born on Jan. 20th and she was unable to go back to work until late September that same yr. She had to have multiple surgeries following the pregnancy, which prevented her from going back to work earlier. Also, after having a baby and the simple fact that she was aging, it became more difficult to lose the necessary weight and look the way she had to look for her job with Disney. Thus, the job transfer that recently occurred.

It appears the borrowers are doing what is necessary to make sure this situation does not happen again. The borrower seems very sincere and is very helpful. She does not plan on being with our loan for an extended period of time as she plans on refinancing either with us or someone else as soon as possible. She is ok with the payment and hopes that it will only be a short time until she can rebuild her credit and move on.

Disneyland and Walt Disney World are spectacular amusement parks that feature exhibits, rides, and shows based on movies by Walt Disney. There, visitors meet such Disney characters as, left to right, Pluto, Goofy, and Mickey Mouse.

The next problem was my wife trying to start a Home business. This did not workout.

11/15/2005 12:36 PM

To Jc_____/ESB@ESB
cc
bcc
Subject

loan

Miles and I spoke to **Mr. and Mrs. Kirkpatrick** and **Mr. Feldman** regarding this transaction. The Kirkpatricks bought the land for $90k in '01. They built the current home and completed it in 4/02 at a cost of $570k. They bought the land with cash and financed the construction. Since then they have done another $30k or so of improvements that has included a 25x15 workshop, paved driveway, front porch and rear patio w/ fire pit.

Their financial issues started when Mr, who was working for the National Missile Defense of Boeing, stopped paying all overtime after 9/11/01. He went from being paid hourly, which included a lot of double and triple time to straight salary. This resulted in a 30% to 40% decrease in his income . Mr is still gainfully employed with Boeing. Mrs did not work then but has since picked a job working for Dress Barn.

Mr. Feldman is a good friend of the Kirkpatricks . **Mr. Feldman** pays everything with cash and has no debt or credit. His main job is as an employee of Marriott is to promote the sales of timeshares. He also is a trainer of birds of prey. He trained the birds used in the Harry Potter movies. The reason **Mr. Feldman** is involved with the Kirkpatricks is to get the cash required to increase the training and to provide a "getaway" where paying customers learn/watch about the birds' hunting practices. This is a unique niche Josh Feldman is involved with and knows it will be a huge money maker hence theKirkpatricksdesire to get Mr Feldman involved with the property and refinance.

Kirkpatrick's home) 435-711-7143
Mr. K work) 801-195-2419
Mrs. K work) 801-624-4304
Feldman cell) 435-919-1524

To: whom it may concern,

Barry and I (Lorie) fell behind with our debts when I received more credit cards than I could handle. Credit Card Companies would send me them and I would except them. I ended up filing for bankrupcy. We tried to save money for our home improvements and then there were other family crisis that would arise for example our oldest daughter at age 18 became pregnant and she had no help from the baby daddy or from his family. So we had to support her and our grandchild. Our family was now a family of seven people in a two bedroom house. Our daughter was employed for a while but she's currently not employed because she can't work weekends because she doesn't have a babysitter on weekends and most of the jobs she apply for need her on weekends.

When Barry got hisself in the same sistuation with too many credit cards they became too overbearing and he co-sign for a car for our son who left him hanging when he didn't make the car payments. What me and Barry plan to do in the future is not to receive anymore credit cards or personal loans. We would just like to pay our mortage payments on time, pay our telephone, electric, etc. and stay away from other creditors. We desperately need extra space. We would like to also use this money to add on an master bedroom and bathroom, we want to renovate our kitchen and put in need doors and windows, new carpet and tiles. We will really appreciate your help in helping us to make this all possible.

Sincerly yours,
Lorie a_____
Barry ____

FORECLOSED!

continues on page 52

19

FOUND by Marina Roberts
Vancleave, MS

I love the notes at the bottom from the
DeathWalkers' selection committee!

—M.R.

DeathWalkers

I, _Levi Deluke_, solemnly swear, that I will be faithful to the brotherhood, and uphold reputation for the Death Walkers. I also agree to take honor in standing for another member. And also, if I am to fail a task, or get caught, I am not to bring the rest of the gang down with me.

Full Name _Levi Micheal Deluke_ Age _12_
Date Of Birth _9-18-92_
Location Of Birth _Rome, NY_
Favorite Animal _Chicken_
Religion _Catholic_
PersonalComments ~~the chicken the was fat~~
I want revenge on Aaron Shook. I'm smart.

I will be serious about Death Walkers _Levi De Luke_

<u>MY NOTES</u>: DEFINETLY A STATEGIC PLANNER. ALSO PHYSICAL. WE'LL SEE HOW IT GOES. NOT SURE HOW SERIOUSLY HE TAKES THE DEATH WALKERS. ALSO HAVE TO DECIDE BETWEEN LEVI AND AARON SHOOK.

21 Balloons Productions

3455 Charing Cross Rd.
Ann Arbor, Mi. 48108

21balloons.com

WELCOME TO 21 BALLOONS!

A NOTE FROM OUR FOUNDER

I GOT THE IDEA to start a production company from a student of mine at Cotton Correctional Facility in Jackson, Michigan named Shorty Smooth Dawson. One day Shorty Smooth showed me a huge chart he'd been working on, laid out over four pieces of notebook paper taped together. "This is Shorty Smooth Productions," he explained to me, and led me through the diagram. His company was broken up into several divisions—music, literature, event entertainment, auto detailing. He'd appointed friends from Cotton to head each department; for example, another student of mine, Omar Leavells-Els, was included on the chart as Director of Casino Operations. As he showed off his handiwork, Shorty Smooth kept bursting with new ideas and scribbling notes down. "Baked Goods!" he said, "That's gonna be one of our primary sources of lucrative revenues. I need just the right man to oversee things." He fixed me with a look.. I thought he was about to offer me the Director of Baked Goods post, but he went another direction. "Davy, you know what," he said, "you should start your own production company. Get a piece of paper and a pen."

Over the next hour, 21 Balloons Productions was born. I took the name from my favorite book in the world, *The 21 Balloons*, by William Pene du Bois. *The 21 Balloons*, published in 1947, tells the story of Professor William Waterman Sherman, a retired schoolteacher in San Francisco who sets out for a full year's journey in a hot-air balloon. On his second day of flight, though, he crash-lands on a remote volcanic island; the book follows his adventures, ending with the noisiest day in the life of any man in history.

Here's how the book begins: "There are two kinds of travel. The usual way is to take the fastest imaginable conveyance along the shortest road. The other way is not to care particularly where you are going or long it will take you, or whether you will get there or not." Du Bois compares the second way of travel to going up in a hot-air balloon—you don't really know where you're headed, but the voyage is bound to be beautiful and amazing. A pretty good way to live, as far as I'm concerned.

One afternoon a few years ago, my own travels took me a city in Colombia called Cali, and in the way that being far from home and smoking weed makes you start reflecting on shit, I started to, well, reflect on shit. And I decided that in my life I want to build twenty-one balloons—one might be a novel, another might be a film, *FOUND Magazine*, that could another. All right, say I've got, like, two or three little kids running around someday, well that'd be two or three balloons right there. I don't know what all of those balloons will be exactly, but I'm excited to find out. And I'm so thrilled that you're taking interest and riding along with me—we'll see where the winds carry us. Thank you, thank you, thank you for joining me on the voyage.

—DAVY

DAVY ROTHBART

21

these photos FOUND by Joe Zucchiatti, Whitehorse, The Yukon

PARKING VIOLATION

FRONT

DT 5001 / 5-06

City of Los Angeles   1044387702

Month	Day	Year	Time	Meter Number	PPD #
06	2⃝ 17	1437			81

5

VIN

LICENS

CA

CHEV
A
FORD
G

LOCATI
43

OFFICER

NOTES

MR

VIOLA

TO THE MOON

Handwritten on back of ticket:

I work Here.
Where am
I suppost
to park
on the
Moon

(printed mailing info, upside down:)
LOS ANGELES CA 90051-1599
P O BOX 512599
CITY OF LOS ANGELES

1044387702

(310) 659-5561
(213) 623-7046 TTY (8-5)

First-Class
Postage
Required

Post Office will
not deliver
without proper
postage.

HALF-A-TICKET   FOUND by Sarah Daniels   Studio City, CA

I DARE YOU

FOUND by Christopher Winkelmann

St. Louis, MO

Handwritten note (left):

You are another
stupid idiot
can you not
read the sign
DO NOT BLOCK
DRIVE WAY

NEXT TIME I
AM GOING TO
HIT YOUR SHIT!

Typed note (right):

Tenants of Bellevue Apartments,
I found this lovely note on my car the other day. Isn't great to know that we have such nice, civil people living among us in our building?

To the author of this note:
I have lived here for 3 years. In that time, people have always parked in the driveway and we have never had any problems. No one's car has ever gotten hit. We have never had any complaints about this until your sorry ass showed up. Maybe if you weren't just some stupid girl you would know how to properly operate your vehicle. Other tenants and I should not have to suffer just because you are too god damned stupid to get your piece of crap car in and out of the garage. Take a driving lesson or two.

P.S. I dare you to "hit my shit". I dare you.

22

SHAME ON YOU FOR TAKING THIS PARKING SPOT WHEN MY SIGNAL WAS CLEARING ON BEFORE YOUR ARRIVAL (= BAD KARMA)

BAD CARMA

This napkin FOUND by Stacy Leech Chicago, IL

ad Karma? No way. Don't you know how confusing your behavior was? Your friend pulled out in front of me. You passed keys. I thought you were pulling out... I guess I was wrong. You just don't know how to park in the Big City!

BACK

SO IN THE FUTURE YOU WON'T PARK SO CLOSE TO THE CAR IN FRONT OF YOU I WANTED TO WRITE YOU THIS NOTE I REALLY WANTED TO BASH IN THE FRONT OF YOUR CAR WITH MINE BUT I THOUGHT THE NOTE WOULD BE BETTER SO THINK BEFORE YOU ACT SO SELFCENTERED

HAVE A NICE DAY

IN THE FUTURE

FOUND by Lori Burtch Long Beach, CA

FLASHCARD

FOUND by Bee Money San Francisco, CA

ONE OF THE MOST IMPORTANT THINGS WE LEARNED WAS:

FRONT

RELENTLESS BICKERING NEVER SOLVED ANYTHING

BACK

This appears to be some kind of interpersonal communication skills flashcard. Not to brag, but I passed that class a long time ago. —B.

FOUND POST-ITS!

Appt 1:30 Fri
Infected toe
Trouble sleeping
Allergy shot
Make pymt.
Thanks.

FOUND by Sam England, Oakland, CA

FREE BEAR
(Not wanted due to emotional sentiments)

FOUND by Kate Cubbler, Asheville, NC

FOUND by Margot Healey, South Pasadena, CA

i have been enjoying trumpets lately.

FOUND by Daniel Costello, Denver, CO

IF He Walked INTO MY LIFE

FOUND by Nikki Kersbergen, Sioux Falls, SD

Move down stairs or some other place

FOUND by Mike Smith, Albuquerque, NM

The Meaning of Life is in the attic

FOUND by Ellen, St. Paul, MN

GOOD NIGHT, SCHMÖÖNCHKIE!
♥, muffin!

FOUND by Hannah Jurs-Allen, Baltimore, M

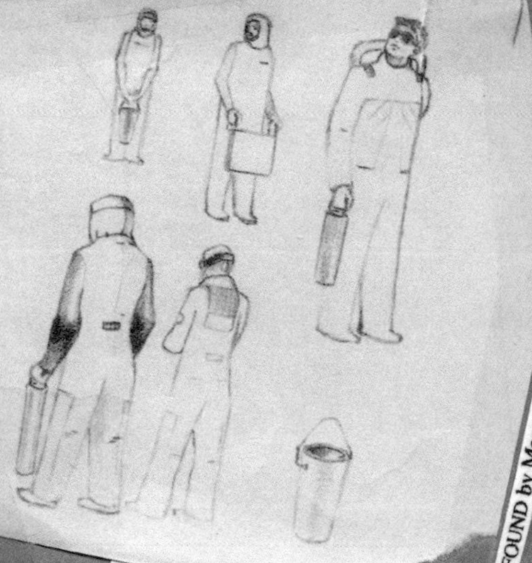

I fell off my bike and smashed my face into the sidewalk yesterday and had to write this paper white on pain meds. I hope it makes sense.

SAVE GLASS & BLACK MESS

274-2925

EVIL

This is Anthonys friend, he asked me to change his voicemail for him because he just got locked up on March 17th, so if your worried or just wondering where hes at — hes up at the montgomery county Jail Alright Bye

Whisky
Beer

CELEBREX.
(CELECOXIB CAPSULES) 100 mg 200 mg

We need to spend more time togeter

sportwagen

kinderwagen

GOODBYE CRUEL WORLD !!!

FINDER'S SPOTLIGHT: MIRANDA JULY

Miranda July is one of my very favorite artists.

I'm a fan of her film *Me and You and Everyone We Know* and a lot of the performance art she's done over the years, but I'm especially spellbound by her short stories.

They contain a combination of sadness and sweetness that resonates with a lot of the found notes we come across.

Knowing her work, it was not a huge surprise but still a great thrill when I heard that Miranda has a wild infatuation with found stuff herself.

She's offered to share a few gems from her own collection—they're scattered over the next dozen pages—and recently I had the chance to chat with her about her favorite finds and the magic of finding.

Davy: Hey Miranda. Looks like you've got an entire treasure chest full of finds. Where'd you find all this stuff?

Miranda: On the streets, on the sidewalk, in the grass. One of my favorite journals I found tucked into an old backpack at Goodwill. Does it count if you buy something at Goodwill and find something inside?

Davy: Absolutely. Goodwill is totally legitimate. The only rule we have with FOUND is that you have to really find it or come across it somewhere. You can't make it up and say you found it. Now, I've got one friend who's a real purist—she told me she thinks it only counts if you find a note blowing down the street. I was being a smart-ass and I was like, "Well, what if it's just laying there?" And she said, "No, it has to be *blowing!*" But finding something at Goodwill, or an old postcard you buy at an antique store—in my mind that still counts without a doubt.

Miranda: Okay, cool. Well, at the Goodwill in Portland, Oregon, I found this diary of a high school girl who wanted desperately to be a good Christian, but was constantly drinking and having sex, then feeling guilty and repentant. She was really in a miserable place. And her little brother keeps breaking into her diary and adding his own bits. At one point he says: *JOEY RULES THE WORLD. HE HOLDS IT IN HIS HANDS.* The girl's got all this heavy stuff on her mind, and Joey busts in so full of life and so free of struggle. Then, on the next page, the girl simply continues on in her little bubbly handwriting with no mention of her brother. She just goes back to her sorrowful tale.

Davy: As we go through the Found mail and read all the finds people have sent in, I always notice how much sadness there seems to be in the world, how many people seem to want things so badly that they're clearly not gonna get, even if they haven't realized it yet themselves.

Miranda: Yeah, I just remembered this other diary I found that's a bit different but has the same heaviness to it. It's this kind of unhappy housewife who writes about the most mundane things, every detail—what she's making for dinner and who picked up the kids from school. Eventually I figured out that she had a code word for sex—when her and her husband got it on, she wouldn't write it out, she just used a code word. It was funny, and she seemed to enjoy sex and look forward to it, but it also felt constrained that she had to keep those moments veiled, even in her own journal.

GHOSTSHRIMP.

CONTINUED ON NEXT PAGE ⟶

Last night I decided to give my life to Jesus. My first big change was to give up Marijuana, alcohol, and cigarrettes. They are no longer a part of my life. I smoked the last bowl and I will take all my pipes and paraphenelia into the counselor tomorrow and see if he can do something to completely destroy all of it - even the pipes. This is kind of a leap of faith. Because you wouldn't believe how hard it is to give up the pipes, my mind is rebelling against that even now. The thing is, I have to get rid of everything that reminds me of that old life, even the mailbox I guess. Oh, man, this is to hard for me. I can't do it.

Last night I watched the twilight zone and it was about hippies grown up. The acid + drugs were no longer a part of their lives - this is the 90's. No more drugs! You wouldn't believe how hard it is for me to quit this habit. I want to hold on to my pipes, and stuff, just for suveniers. But I do realize that if I do make that step it will be easier to refuse intoxicants in the future. I'm going to put an insert in this journal. Something that spoke to me when I was high. and before.

The world is totally sensationalized. And its ok to dream but not to live in your dreams + not face the real problems of life.

I'M __NOT__ STUPID! I AM SMART !!! AND I __WILL__ DO WELL, WITH GOD'S HELP. I WILL __NOT FAIL__!

sm

Joey rales the world. He has it in his hand. He can Destroy Sereina Joey Rules

He killed The strogest Man in the World. I carys aroud granades.

CONTINUED ON NEXT PAGE *!!!*

29

Miranda (continued): There's this sense of hopeless repetition when you're just living your life, day after day, stuck in that certain kind of low feeling. This journal—nothing in the world could capture this sad feeling more. I've always loved books where people are driven toward something, and the whole book seems to be leading up to it, and then nothing happens. And a lot of people live lives like that. I try to make sure I've always got something to look forward to. Part of my drive to always have a bunch of different projects going is so I'll always have something to be excited about.

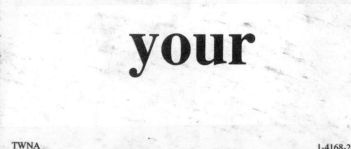

TWNA   1-4168-2810-9

Davy: So finding these journals—and maybe trying to avoid that brooding feeling that's in them—has inspired you to make art?

Miranda: Yeah, but the funny thing is that in most of my art I end up trying to capture that feeling of heaviness and sameness, the feeling that nothing is going to change. And sometimes when I'm writing and my writing's not going very well, I begin to feel desperate. I'll take a walk around the block, and something I see—or a conversation I overhear—or something I find on the ground—always provides a spark. These found notes, they're like these perfect little artifacts: *Oh look! People are sad. I am sad.* It's like we're all aliens, and we need to collect these things as reminders of what it's like to be human.

Davy: Each find has its own unique brew of emotion and story, and you just feel like you're touching people so intimately when you read journals like these.

'It's like we're all aliens, and we need to collect these things as reminders of what it's like to be human.'

TWNA   1-4168-2810-9

Cinthya Garcia   5-24-99

Something I will always remember.

Miranda: I'm the sort of person, whenever I'm walking, I always have to turn over each piece of paper I see, and make sure the secrets of the universe aren't written on the other side.

Davy: Yeah, I feel like the secrets of the universe are more likely to be laying on a scrap of paper in the gutter than in a classroom or a library.

Miranda: It's funny, before I made my first movie, *Me and You and Everyone We Know*, I'd decided that in the last scene this guy would put a picture of flowers up in this tree. I needed just the right picture of flowers, so I went down the street from where I live to a place called the Millenium Thrift Store. This isn't your typical thrift store—it's basically a dumping ground for smelly garbage, filled with dirty, stained mattresses and lots of things you'd never ever want. They didn't have any pictures of flowers, but I saw one of a bird sitting in a tree and bought it for a quarter.

The guy at the register was trying to tell me in Spanish what kind of bird it was, but I was confused for a minute. Just as I was heading out the door, I realized that he was saying it was a quail. I smiled at him and for some reason tried to walk out of the store holding the picture the way a quail would. I remember thinking to myself, "Why am I doing this?" But then it struck me that something weird and interesting was happening, and that this was a moment I needed to pay attention to. I'd call it a *found* moment. The fact that I'd done this weird thing and that the guy had even seemed to get what I was doing was a tipoff that I was onto something. So I took this picture of the bird in a tree and put it in a tree, and it turned out to be a small, nice moment in my movie that wouldn't have happened otherwise.

Davy: You wanted a picture of flowers, but they had a picture of a bird, so of course a bird is what was right.

Miranda: Exactly! I try to keep all of my art and all of my life flexible enough that I can allow in these moments of accidental luck and inspiration.

Davy: I feel like I try to live my life in the same sort of way—taking value in the unexpected, and trying not to be too married to any one idea. There's this serendipity to finding things, it can feel magical.

Miranda: Yeah, but I don't think of it as fate or that the universe is trying to tell me something. I'm telling myself it. It's not about magic, it's just the way things really are. It's real. Like a table. It's concrete. It's already existing. You just have to be aware. We look for information to come to us in precise and logical ways, but you have to be open to moments like this. You have to practice being methodically open the way you would practice anything else, like math.

Davy: Picking up pieces of paper off the ground is a way of staying in practice.

31

CONTINUED ON NEXT PAGE →

Des,

I have not been able to stop thinking about you and what we talked about since yesterday, 4ᵗʰ period. I feel so goddam helpless when it comes to helping you with your problems— I want to very much.

We were talking yesterday about suicide, well, the way I see it, there are only two reasons why a person would want to do that

#1. They feel worthless

#2. They feel they have nothing to live for.

I'm telling you the truth when I say that I care about you more than you ever may realize, and if you ever feel either of those two ways, think about me. Call me. Because I swear that I will always be here for you and you'll alway have someone to turn to.

It's kind of funny, assholes like Jake have a <u>chance</u> to date a nearly perfect person, and treat her like a Goddess; and people like me get to be their friend. Well, I don't mind, I won't be lonesome forever, (I Hope).

Anyway, you know that little freshman girl that likes me? Well, she was accusing me of hanging all over some girl and

asking her permission to ~~go~~ go to the
movies with her. she hasn't told me
that to my face, but she told a "friend"
of mine and he told me about it.
she's acting like were going out, and
I told her "no" like two weeks ago
when she asked me out!
   Anyway I figured you shuld know
about all those things I wrote at
the beginning of this note. (EVERY WORD
I said is the truth. I promise you
on my honor that I will never lie
to you.)

Love Always & Forever

Erik

Miranda: Yeah, and if you stick to the practice of picking up each little scrap, good things will come. A lot of the time it's just a napkin or a receipt or something boring, but that doesn't matter, you're not dumb for turning it over.

Davy: And sometimes even the receipts are pretty cool. We got a couple of great ones recently. My friend Tucker found a receipt that just had four items on it: *Gun, gun, ski mask, Nerds.* And a month later, he found another receipt that said *Chicken ramen noodes, chicken ramen noodles, chicken ramen noodles, chicken ramen noodles, chicken ramen noodles, chicken ramen noodles, 12-pack lubricated condoms.*

Miranda: Sounds interesting! Though I got to say it seems like there's less good Found stuff here in L.A. than in Portland, where I used to live. Maybe there's less people dropping things here?

Davy: Yeah, maybe it's more of a place where people get around by car, so less people are dropping things.

Miranda: Well, it's probably because *I'm* not walking. If you're not walking or on your bike, you're less likely to find stuff.

Davy: We do get some great stuff from L.A., though. Maybe not as much as Portland. Portland is hugely fertile territory for Found stuff.

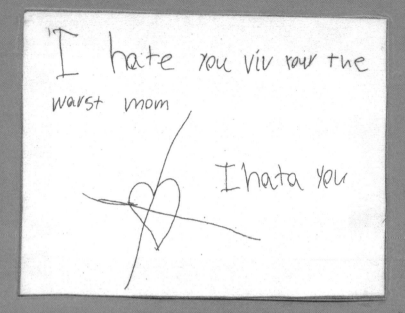

Miranda: Yeah, Portland's a finder's paradise, and when I lived there I always walked everywhere. I'd find crazy-people writings in great abundance. Maybe the crazy people here in L.A. aren't as literate. They don't put pen to paper, they just speak their thoughts.

Davy: They have TV shows.

Miranda: True! I think, ultimately, that crazy-people writing—like the kind you find at Kinko's—sometimes it's so crazy it all kind of seems the same.

Davy: I know what you mean. Sometimes it's just the mental illness speaking and you can't relate to it the way you can relate to other found notes. Let me ask you something—you said you always pick stuff up or turn it over with your foot... Do you ever pick something up and then if it's not that interesting you feel like you can't just put it down again 'cause that would be littering?

Miranda: Yeah! I'll sometimes carry it with me for a little while and then put it down with great deliberation, like I'm leaving it for someone to pick up later. My boyfriend always laughs about it.

Davy: Does your boyfriend think you're weird for picking up trash?

Miranda: No, he gets it. I grew up in Berkeley and he grew up in Santa Barbara—it's dirtier in Berkeley, so I've always been finding stuff, but he still appreciates it all. I don't think I could date someone who doesn't.

'It's not about magic, it's just the way things really are. It's real. Like a table.'

My baby
Whats Up, I heard that you called me yesterday, Man I got my sister pissed. Because the day I told you I didnt know if I should go to the battle I heard that my crew lost and that my sister tried to start a fight with them. So I told my sister that I wanted to battle her in this place called "the claim" In Las Vegas. And we beat her crew and got $500 on Saturday. You left early on Friday huh because. I had to go to the Attendance office to Usee Mr. Von Wooster and your mom was gone. I'm sorry I didnt answer your call Its cause I was in another car. That was funny what I did On the Roller Coaster in Circus Circus. When the camera took a picture I flicked it off y me salio a picture of. a clown. I was gonna call u but I was out on the streets. I bet u were in Church almost all day yesterday. I got to go back next week to help out. All right I gotta go. If you want we could talk later. If you want.
Love Always
Your babyboy
Lil URL
U-Dee

Davy: How old were you when you first started collecting Found stuff?

Miranda: Well, when I was a kid, I used to religiously ask my dad if I could go through his trash. He'd grudgingly allow me to sift through his junk mail, old notes, lists, and abandoned, half-finished letters. His handwriting was eerie and intense, like a disturbed child's, but reading through his discarded papers, I got this sense for the tiny, strange details of his life. It became a way to find intimacy with him.

Davy: I remember being fascinated with my dad's study. The place was chaotic, and we weren't allowed in there, me and my brothers, but when my dad was out of the house we'd go spelunking in there and sift through his shit. Reading his papers and looking at all of his little trinkets and newspaper clippings and ancient *Playboys*, it was a strange and awesome feeling. It was like I was getting to know him as a person in the world and not just my dad. Looking at Found letters still gives me that same thrill.

Miranda: Finding stuff, it's like a form of people watching.

Davy: Yeah, my mom calls it 'people watching on paper.' Miranda, will you share some more finds with us soon? We'll put a couple new favorites in the next issue.

Miranda: For sure. Count on it!

Miranda July's amazing book of stories is called *No One Belongs Here More Than You.* Check out lots more of her awesome work at **www.MirandaJuly.com.**

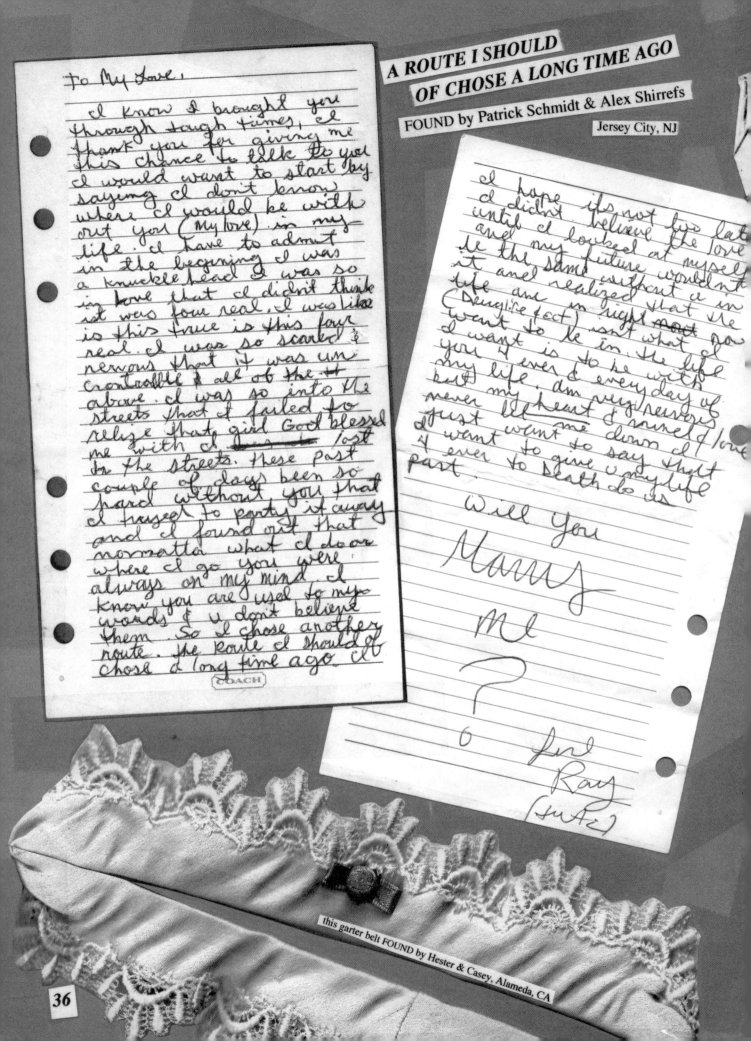

To My Love,

I know I brought you through tough times, I thank you for giving me this chance to talk to you I would want to start by saying I don't know where I would be without you (my love) in my life. I have to admit in the beginning I was a knuckle head I was so in love that I didn't think it was four real. I was like is this true is this four real. I was so scared & nervous that it was uncontrollable & all of the above. I was so into the streets that I failed to relize that girl God blessed me with I ~~~ lost in the streets. these past couple of days been so hard without you that I tryed to party it away and I found out that no matta what I do or where I go you were always on my mind. I know you are used to my words & u don't believe them. So I chose another route. The route I should of chose a long time ago. I

COACH

I hope its not too late I didn't believe the love untill I looked at myself and my future would be the same without it and realized that we are in right not you (Seng'ire fact) isn't what I want to be in. The life I want is to be with you 4 ever & every day of my life. I am very serious but my heart & mind & love never let me down I just went to say that I went to give u my life 4 ever to death do us part.

Will You

Marry

Me

?

O

for
Ray
(sure)

this garter belt FOUND by Hester & Casey, Alameda, CA

10-29-06

Dear Management and Office Depot,

The time has come for my time with Office Depot to ___ ___ ___ ve of all ___ that the management especially Theresa and Rocky. There ___ ___ ___t of change here within the last year, obviously with a remodel change of management, and a constant change of associates.

Unfortunately, as much as some of the days have been very fun and wonderful, I must move on. The season of my unhappiness here cannot go on. I am very sorry. I thank you for the opportunity to be an associate.

Sincerely,

Amanda Reed

Amanda Reed

THE SEASON OF MY UNHAPPINESS

FOUND by Cat Baldwin

at the University of Oregon Eugene, OR

INSIDE OF FOLDED-UP NOTE   OUTSIDE

— switch cars

Full City
Papa John's
McDonald
Theater

MOVIN' ON

FOUND by Kathryn Lachey & Nolan

at Illinois Wesleyan University   Bloomington, IL

Dear Suburban Pediatrics,

I believe the time has come when, as a twenty-one-year-old, I have to move on. I've been coming here since I could fit on the infant scale and I'd say I enjoyed coming in over the years.

Please have my medical file ready for pickup tomorrow morning. I'm coming back for Thanksgiving break and there is something that I want my new physician to see.

Thanks for Everything,

John O'Malley

37

Attention Crystal Lake:

I'd hate to disappoint, and so I'm offering my letter of resignation.

To be frank, to-the-point, non-skirting, not backward at coming forward, etcetera, etcetera, this town, and—more precisely—this water park, are toxicities to me. Never in my life have I seen such abundance and excess equate to such little thoughtfulness and character. Perhaps I'm aboveboard, perhaps I'm puerile, but it seems to me that clichés often be*come* clichés for a reason. Your suburb, without a shadow of a doubt, proves what I've always suspected: the more affluent the people, the more disaffected their values. If Crystal Lake represents, rather fairly, East Brunswick, then I've encountered, during the course of two summers, enough phony Phils and Lady Mucks to last me several lifetimes. Your obsession with material, gossip, image, and all rather irrelevant, cursory matters, along with your investment in *quantity* as opposed to quality, is nauseating and abhorrent. The great majority of you will never rise above the fickle tastes of magazine-land, not only because you're too stupid, apathetic and complacent, but because, in all your material comfort, you'll never know or possess *true* hunger. You'll never be anything more than cookie-cutter, a nickel-a-dozen, clearance sale sheeple. In the end, your tree-lined suburb, trendy clothes, cell phones, good teeth, expensive colleges will not protect you or offer absolution, but instead leave you just where you belong: swimming in obscurity; another zombie sitting in rush-hour traffic listening to traffic reports and weather memorandums, spilling coffee on your lap, married to someone you despise, making six figures a year with a pot belly big enough to deep-six a ship.

My apologies, in advance, to those of you I've grown quite fond of, to those of you who've become the object of my adoration. With autumn, and ultimately winter, closing in, I'll often think of you and wonder what you're reading, what you're watching and from where you're doing it. It's a great comfort to me knowing that there are people out there who, despite what they've been told, do not regard the downtrodden as malignant, but instead look at them as potential. Heaven help me, but the downtrodden *are* the potential; the downtrodden possess a hunger and desperation that God himself couldn't manufacture, and *that*, pal, is what stardust is made of.

In closing, I'll send you my best and hope that the rest of your summer is as fulfilling as carrying a really heavy garbage bag from one end of Crystal Lake to the other without tearing a ligament in your arm. It's mid-August, and I believe that us vagabonds have gotten our wish: it's hot as a neutron bomb, and the stars are high and blurred. Oh, the summer—the sweet, sweet summer…it's goddamn immortal.

All best,

M. DYLAN RASKIN

The story behind this find is strange but true. For the last 6 summers I've worked at a water park called Crystal Springs as a lifeguard. This past summer a new guy took over as the maintenance crew leader. His name was Dylan and he was older than the rest of us, around 25. He quickly became one of the most popular people around; everyone wanted to be his friend because he was awesome and not like the rest of the people in this town. He was smart, funny, and charming, and had the greatest, most hysterical stories. Sometimes he'd have a group of 30 lifeguards around him on the edge of their seats as he told one of his stories about life in Queens, NY, where he was from. From what I understand, he was crashing on his cousin's couch for the summer in East Brunswick.

Rumors started to go around that our very popular co-worker Dylan was actually the author of two published books, one of which many of us were reading for English class—Little New York Bastard. No one ever wanted to ask him directly, but we all figured out that he was actually the guy from his picture on the back of his books. Well, one day at work some lifeguard decided to be a jerk and ask him about it. I don't know how Dylan responded in that moment, but the next day Crystal Springs was littered with copies of his resignation letter. "Crystal Lake" is a reference to the movie Friday the 13th, which he always talked about. I'll never forget Dylan or the effect he had on this town.

—C.P.

this photo FOUND in a garage sale paperback of James Joyce's *Ulysses* by Mark and Jules, Kalamazoo, MI

IT'S UP TO YOU.

You can spend your days lying in the grass smoking cigarettes, drinking Michelobs, palming volleyballs, and staring maniacally at your friends.

Or... you can

READ THIS BOOK!!

"Davy writes with his whole heart. These stories are crushing."
—ARTHUR MILLER

"...nny, flashy . . . a great whirlwind."
—*Los Angeles Times*

"It's always exciting to discover a talented new writer. Davy writes with such energy, wit, and heart."
—Judy Blume

THE LONE SURFER OF MONTANA, KANSAS

STORIES

DAVY ROTHBART
AUTHOR OF THE NATIONAL BESTSELLER *FOUND*

A book of stories from the creator of *Found!*

Much like the lost, tossed, and forgotten items Davy Rothbart collects in his acclaimed magazine *Found*, *The Lone Surfer of Montana, Kansas* captures the oddity, poetry, and dignity of everyday life.

"Like Kerouac's best novels, these stories are breezy and energetic dispatches from obscure corners of the country. Rothbart mines his material to heartbreaking effect."
—*The Washington Post*

TOUCHSTONE
A Division of Simon & Schuster
A CBS COMPANY

2201 Carmelina Ave
Los Angeles, CA 90064
310-826-62

April 15, 2006

RESIDENTS, eh?

No problem!
Do your Best!
Good luck!

Dear Homeowners and Residence of North Beach,

I would like to introduce MJZ Productions, a film production company specializing in commercial media. We are filming a television commercial for Fruit of the Loom.

In coordination with the Film Commission, The San Francisco Police Department and the Mayors Office, we will be filming in your neighborhood on April 18th, April 19th and April 20th, 2006 between the hours of 7 AM and 8 PM.

Avenue

We will be posting NO PARKING SIGNS in the vicinity of Filbert St, Union St. As well as on Grant ~~Street~~. Please observe these signs, as we need to be able to place the camera and equipment trucks in very specific places. As well as, emptying the streets of pedestrian vehicles to create the illusion of an empty neighborhood.

If you have any special concerns please feel free to contact us so we help alleviate any issue that may cause disruptions to your day.

Thanking you in advance for your assistance.

Sincerely,

This not an empty
neighborhood —
pack up your illusions
and go back to L.A.
Thank you
A resident of 40 yrs

Michael Raziano
Locations Manager
415-388-78 9.

Recently my friend and I were walking down the street and saw a notice posted to a residence announcing that a production company would be filming a Fruit of the Loom commercial nearby. The sign offered a telephone number to call if anyone had special concerns, so we memorized the number and along with a co-worker left 3 messages stating our concerns regarding a fear of large, talking fruit, distress for the lack of fruit diversity (I've seen your apples and grapes but would you please consider taking this opportunity to expand to citrus, bananas, mangoes, avocado?) and an appeal from an agent to consider casting a client for the role of Pear (although he's been working on his kiwi and really the kid is golden, he can do anything.)

The next day we found the same notice for the commercial posted on a different residence. Apparently those who actually do live close by chose to add their concerns directly to the posting, ranging from correcting the notice to enthusiastic support to the harsh admonishment that San Francisco is no place for illusions. —Paula

FRUIT OF THE LOOM

FOUND by Paula

San Francisco, CA

drawing FOUND by Sara Huston,
San Francisco, CA

A CHILD TO CALL MY OWN
FOUND by Bradley Monton

Kauai, Hawaii

I found this note in a demolished 2007 Honda
Fit abandoned on the side of a rural road. —B.M.

1·15·06

dear god,
i turn to you for everything
when things go bad you shine your light
when im mad at the world
you make things better
but who do i turn to
when im mad at you.
this happened again
And i dont know why
you would take my pride & joy
~~you took~~ you took away my life
i didnt even know i had another life
in me
till the blood flowed and along came
the pain

then the doctors said "Ms. Fernandez, were
sorry to say, but you just had a
misscarriage today." (11·14·06)
god, why would you let me go through this pain
and suffering?
why would you take my child away from me?
who do i turn to
when im mad at you?

who do i turn
to when
im mad at
you?

WHY DID YOU TAKE MY CHILD?

WHY

CONTINUED →

yesterday i woke up
Just another ordinary day
till i looked on the bed
& Felt the pain, wishing it would go away.

11-15-06

Went to the doctor,
they sent me to the ER
then i heard something that made me flip-out.
i keep a smile, didn't want anybody to know
but the pain just wouldn't stop.
i pop a pill to make the pain go away
i slept all day with a baby in my dream
i wake up - stund.
the pain continues, the blood still flows
i try to be happy
but anger in my heart still lingers.
all my life now,
i'll be Questioning what it would be
like with the child in my arms.
a child to call my own.

why me?
what did i do to deserve this....

AGAIN

Jamie Lee

There was a time
my ♡ belonged to
Aaron.
but now...
my ♡ belongs to
Stephen.

Fish   Honey Poultry   KAUAI
        Sugar   Sugar
        Cane   Cane
                Fruit
    Sheep
Cattle NIIHAU   Fish

First misscarriage:
~~●~~ August 27, 2009
(3 months)

second misscarriage:
November 13, 2009
(1 month)

I dont want a third
misscarriage
please....
i beg of you
please god.
let this be the
last one!!!!!
please...
♥always
Jam Lee

The names i chose:
girl- akiko kim
boy- alijah kim

[Surprise]
Didnt even know...

→ who's the daddy?

Aaron or Stephen?

↓   ↓
Never use   the First
condom   time never
but pulls   use condom
out except   but pulled
one time.   out. used condoms
                   after...

WTF!

maybe..
(Just maybe)
this is a sign
that im not
meant to have a
child, but the
pain is so bad.

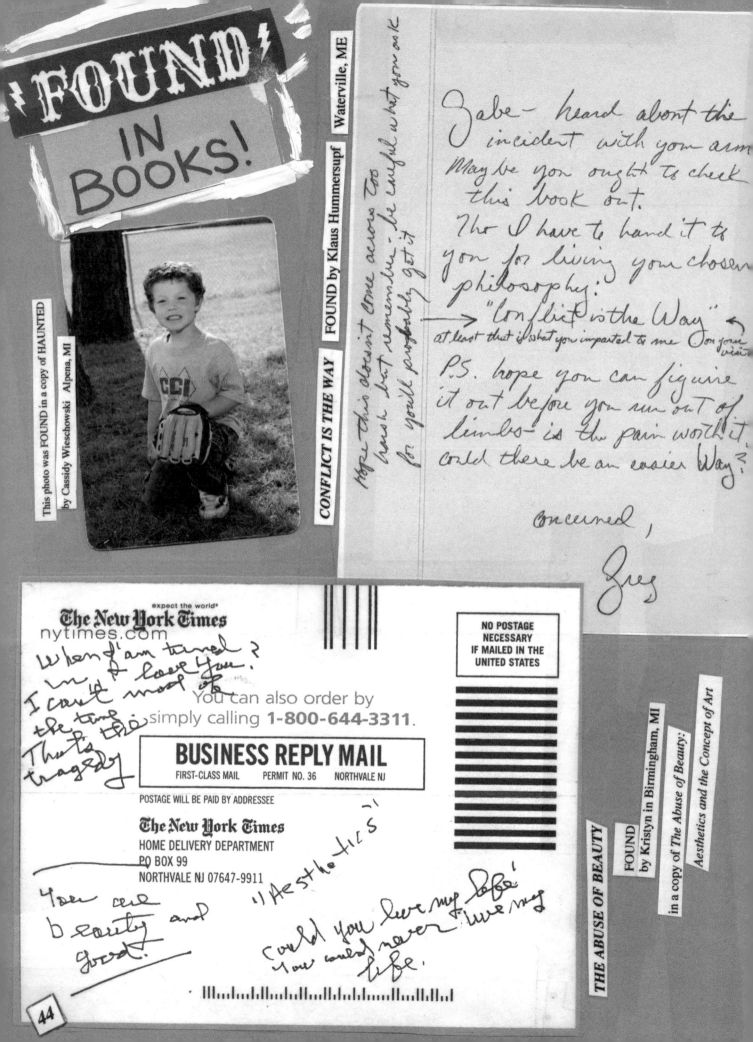

FOUND IN BOOKS!

This photo was FOUND in a copy of HAUNTED
by Cassidy Wieschowski   Alpena, MI

CONFLICT IS THE WAY

FOUND by Klaus Hummersupf   **Waterville, ME**

Hope this doesn't come across too
harsh but remember - be careful what you ask
for you'll probably get it

Gabe- heard about the
incident with your arm
Maybe you ought to check
this book out.
Tho I have to hand it to
you for living your chosen
philosophy:
→ "Conflict is the Way" ←
at least that is what you imparted to me on your visit

P.S. hope you can figure
it out before you run out of
limbs - is the pain worth it
could there be an easier Way?

concerned,

Greg

The New York Times
nytimes.com

When I am turned
in, I lose you.
I can't mop up
the time.
That's the
tragedy

You can also order by
simply calling **1-800-644-3311**.

BUSINESS REPLY MAIL
FIRST-CLASS MAIL   PERMIT NO. 36   NORTHVALE NJ

POSTAGE WILL BE PAID BY ADDRESSEE

The New York Times
HOME DELIVERY DEPARTMENT
PO BOX 99
NORTHVALE NJ 07647-9911

NO POSTAGE
NECESSARY
IF MAILED IN THE
UNITED STATES

You see
beauty and
good!

"Aesthetics"

could you save my life
you could never save my
life.

THE ABUSE OF BEAUTY

FOUND by Kristyn in Birmingham, MI

in a copy of The Abuse of Beauty:
Aesthetics and the Concept of Art

44

FOUND by Ksenija Simic   Tucson, AZ

This letter was discovered inside of a Joseph Campbell book at a used bookstore.

Happy Birthday and happy Fathers's Day Dad,

It isn't often that I take the time to write. Usually because I don't have much to say, or really don't know how to say it. But these two days are special times for me, and since I don't know what to give you, I thought I would take this time to share some of my thoughts.

When I came to visit last October, it was an awkward attempt to spend time with you and get to know you a bit better than I do. While we may not have gotten any closer than we were before, it was a marvelous time for me and I feel a real need to spend more time with my father. You see, I don't believe that Anne and I really got to know our parents very well, least of all, our father. I am at the age where it is becoming more important to me to do this and the time to do it seems to slip away faster than I care to admit.

What brings this on is the time I have been spending in a men's group for the last year and a half. The same kind of men's group that has been sweeping the nation for the last few years kind of like the women's movement did back in the 60's. We have been learning about ourselves as men growing up in "modern" society and culture, and why we feel the way we do, especially about women. I think this is real good stuff and It has really helped me get a handle on my feelings, my anger, and my loneliness. This is the first time I have ever been able to talk with other men in ways I normally protect or hide from the rest of the world. It is the work we do in this group that has helped me understand part of the world that my grandfathers, you and now I grew up in. This is going to really help Josh, for there is a cycle that needs to be broken, and a heritage that must be honored and passed on. There is a bond between fathers and their sons that I want to help strengthen.

So my Birthday wish is for more chances to see each other and get to share each other's lives. I started to buy this book for me. As I was thumbing through it, the thoughts of what am I going to get for Dad along with how much I would like to share this with you came to mind. So I bought one for you reflecting on the times that you gave me the books that were important or useful to you.

I've been reading books similar to this one to bring up issues that we can talk about and explore in the group. This is the kind of book that can be left on the night table to read a couple of pages each night before drifting off to sleep which is what I plan to do. And each night as I read this book, I'll be thinking of you doing the same thing, wondering what you think about as you read these passages.

I love you Dad. Have a wonderful birthday and happy Father's day. Hope to see you soon.

Charlene
     I'd like TO See you again SomeTime
But if you don't Think thats possible Then
at least Send me your addless if you leave
School. Like I said I'll Start Sending you
money as Soon as I know your getting My leTTers.
     I know you change alot and I dont
like you to much right now, ~~M~~ but
I STILL love you and always will even
if That means only being friends
     Please Let Me Know Whare you are Mark

I hope everything worked out, where ever Mark and Charlene ended up. I've kept this note for three years and always imagined a happy ending and hope it came true!   -J.C.

FOUND Magazine. A bad thing will happen if you don't read it!

IF YOU LEAVE SCHOOL

FOUND in a Stephen King book

by Jennine C.   Warrenville, IL

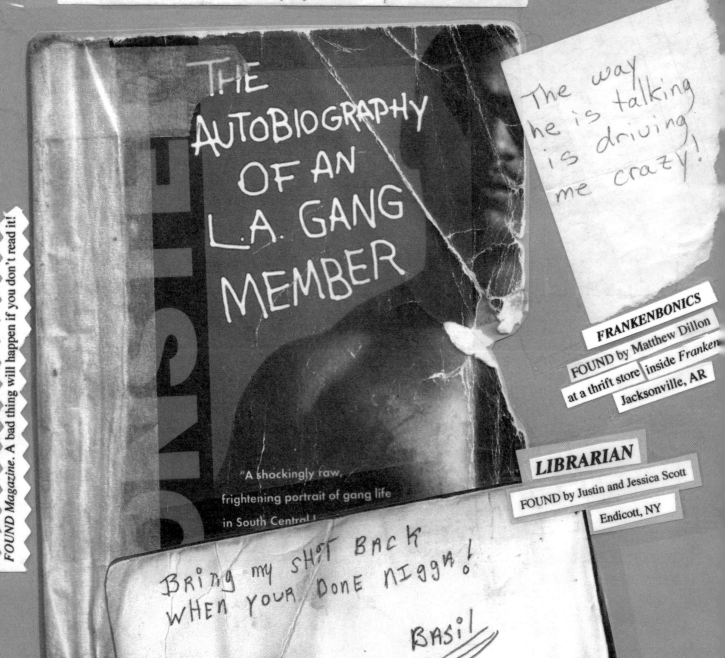

THE
AUTOBIOGRAPHY
OF AN
L.A. GANG
MEMBER

"A shockingly raw,
frightening portrait of gang life
in South Central L

Bring my SHIT BACK
WHEN YOUR DONE NIGGa!

BASIL

The way
he is talking
is driving
me crazy!

FRANKENBONICS

FOUND by Matthew Dillon
at a thrift store inside Franken
Jacksonville, AR

LIBRARIAN

FOUND by Justin and Jessica Scott
Endicott, NY

FOUND by Justin Gardner   Louisville, KY

Hello I am T.A. Read This Book
because it is very inportent
So Read it!   A bad thing
T.A. was here will happen
if you do not
Feb. 15, 2008 // Read it

I Dont Know what Im
feeling right now I mean
I love Jason but y is
Danielle + Ashley mad at me
for liking him so what if
we like eachother

Love is it
a good thing
or not

me?

now //

THE BOY THAT LIVES IN MY MOUTH

Chuckie Cheese
1-800-chuckie-Fun
call-
The cool way to
be a kid.

IN MY LIFE

FOUND by Lindsey Simard

Osh Kosh, WI

2006

2013

Danyelle Dougherty
Paper 3
Human Behavior
November 11, 2005

My Life

In 2014 I was living in Phoenix, Arizona married to Chris Parker. Chris and I met at the school where I had been working at for the past 5 years as the school counselor, Chris was the second grade teacher at the time. It was love at first sight when we met, I knew that I wanted to spend the rest of my life with him. We only dated for 3 months until he asked for my hand in marriage. That is one day of my life I will never forget. He took me out for dinner and as he led me to the table, there sat a dozen roses. As I leaned over to smell the beautiful flower I saw the ring placed on the middle rose. The world seemed to stop along with my heart. The next thing I known Chris is on one knee asked me to marry him. It felt like 10 minutes that I stood there is awe and amazement until I blurted out the words that changed the rest of my life, "YES!! OF COURSE!" Chris and I had a rather short engagement of 9 months before we decide to wed on June 21, 2013. Chris and I were married for 2 years before I gave birth to our little baby boy. Bailey was born August 14, 2015. He was the light of our lives.

On June 8th 2024 Chris and I were still employed at Somerset Elementary School. We had such a love for our work. Our hearts went out to all the unfortunate children and we wanted to be a positive influence in their lives. This was a hard point i my life because I remembered being young and youthful looking at 40 year olds and thinking that they were "old." I don't feel a day over 21. Bailey was 18 years old and heading off to college. This was a very big obstacle of Chris and especially me to

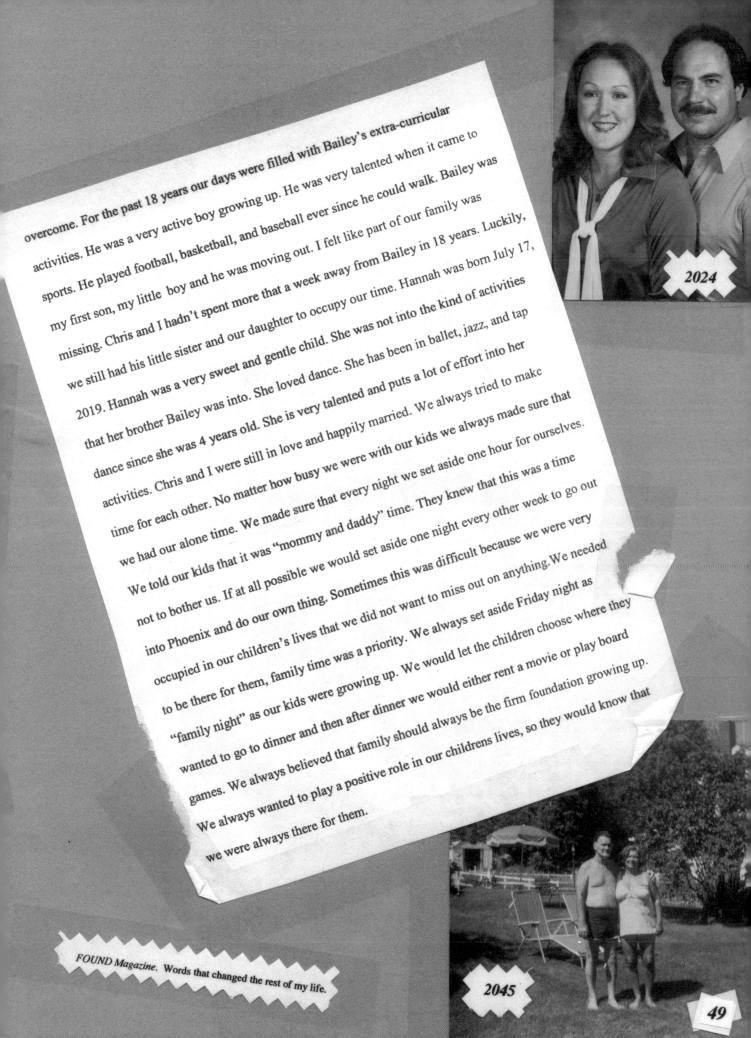

overcome. For the past 18 years our days were filled with Bailey's extra-curricular activities. He was a very active boy growing up. He was very talented when it came to sports. He played football, basketball, and baseball ever since he could walk. Bailey was my first son, my little boy and he was moving out. I felt like part of our family was missing. Chris and I hadn't spent more that a week away from Bailey in 18 years. Luckily, we still had his little sister and our daughter to occupy our time. Hannah was born July 17, 2019. Hannah was a very sweet and gentle child. She was not into the kind of activities that her brother Bailey was into. She loved dance. She has been in ballet, jazz, and tap dance since she was 4 years old. She is very talented and puts a lot of effort into her activities. Chris and I were still in love and happily married. We always tried to make time for each other. No matter how busy we were with our kids we always made sure that we had our alone time. We made sure that every night we set aside one hour for ourselves. We told our kids that it was "mommy and daddy" time. They knew that this was a time not to bother us. If at all possible we would set aside one night every other week to go out into Phoenix and do our own thing. Sometimes this was difficult because we were very occupied in our children's lives that we did not want to miss out on anything. We needed to be there for them, family time was a priority. We always set aside Friday night as "family night" as our kids were growing up. We would let the children choose where they wanted to go to dinner and then after dinner we would either rent a movie or play board games. We always believed that family should always be the firm foundation growing up. We always wanted to play a positive role in our childrens lives, so they would know that we were always there for them.

2024

2045

FOUND Magazine. Words that changed the rest of my life.

49

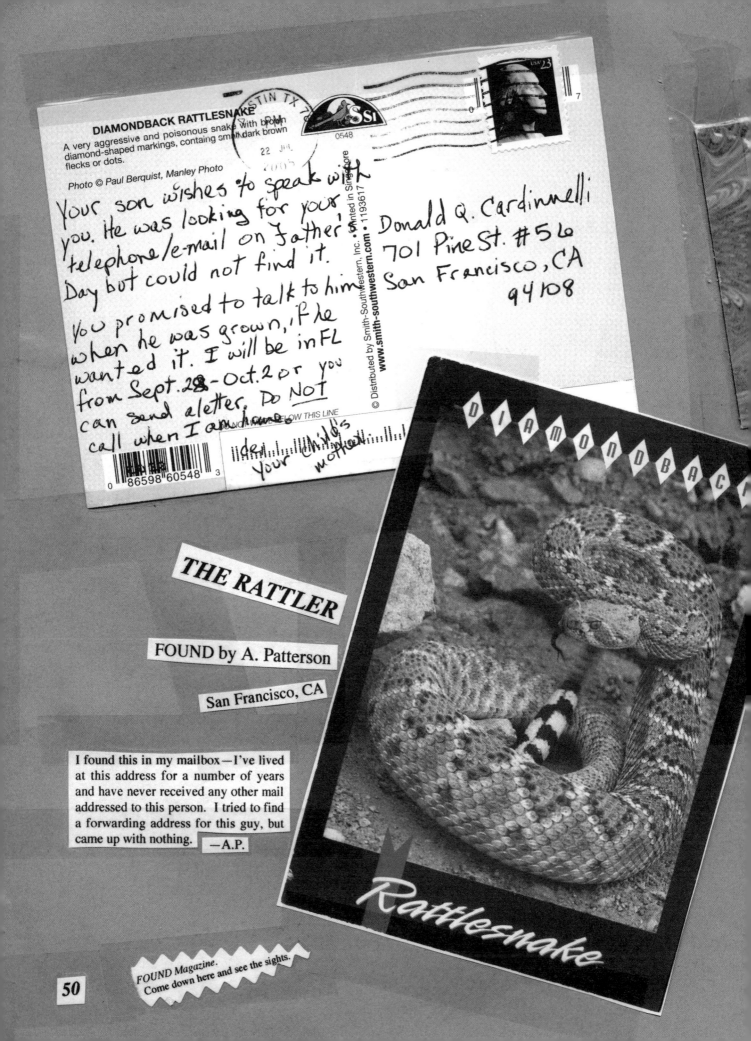

DIAMONDBACK RATTLESNAKE
A very aggressive and poisonous snake with brown
diamond-shaped markings, containg small dark brown
flecks or dots.

Photo © Paul Berquist, Manley Photo

AUSTIN TX
22 JUL 2005
0548

USA 23

Your son wishes to speak with
you. He was looking for your
telephone/e-mail on Father's
Day but could not find it.

You promised to talk to him
when he was grown, if he
wanted it. I will be in FL
from Sept. 28 - Oct. 2 or you
can send a letter. DO NOT
call when I am home.

Your child's mother

Donald Q. Cardinmelli
701 Pine St. #56
San Francisco, CA
94108

0 86598 60548 3

DISTRIBUTED BY SMITH-SOUTHWESTERN, INC. • PRINTED IN Singapore
www.smith-southwestern.com • 1193617

THE RATTLER

FOUND by A. Patterson

San Francisco, CA

I found this in my mailbox—I've lived
at this address for a number of years
and have never received any other mail
addressed to this person. I tried to find
a forwarding address for this guy, but
came up with nothing.   —A.P.

DIAMONDBACK

Rattlesnake

*FOUND Magazine.
Come down here and see the sights.*

All Souls Day
Remembrance

In the Holy Sacrifice of the Mass, on All Souls Day, please remember the souls of:

1. ~~Kit~~ Josh
2. Priscilla
3. Cans
4. ~~Pig~~ Jeg Pig
5. _____

6. _____
7. _____
8. _____
9. _____
10. _____

Name _____
Address _____
Amount $ _____

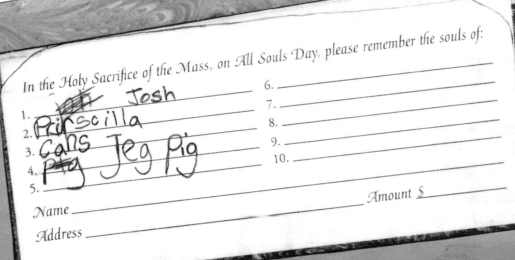

Bag Pipes

Sunday   Insect Bite
Africa   Indian
~~Kiss an insect ass~~

MUSTACHE
MONOGRAM
TELLTALE
CLAM BAKE
BEESTING
BASEBALL

FORECLOSED!

continued from page 19

RE: Narrative on Financial History of James G. MacDougal

In August, 1996 I was employed in Chicago at a private school for behavior disordered youths as a case manager/advocate. I was employed there for 19 years and with one weeks notice they let my whole team go. At that point in time, I was also attending Loyola University graduate school for Social Work in my last year. I was 42 years old and had 4 children and my wife at home. Within a weeks time my wife also got news that she had breast cancer. She had surgery and has recovered but it took a lot out of both of us. My wife has held her job with Electromotive Division of GM (now Electromotive Diesel) for 27 years. We decided in 1996, that somehow I would finish grad school. I was assigned to Hines VA hospital as a social work intern working with substance abuse veterans. For this, I was paid a stipend of $100/week. I also worked part time jobs teaching DUI class for the Cook County Court, counselor with Midwest Family Services and in the evening as a laborer with UPS. Despite the fact that this became a regular 20 hour day, I only was making half the money that I had made before I was laid off. I also later took on a position as graduate assistant at Loyola which helped along with my veteran benefits to pay the rest of my tuition. This went on for about a year until I graduated with a Masters Degree in Social Work. I was hired the day after graduation in 1997 to work with another youth agency. It was a nice job but again paid about $8000 less per year than I was receiving in 1996. I did this job for 2 years while constantly applying for positions at Hines VA where I had interned. Hines hired me in 1999 initially again at $8000 less than the job I had lost but with the promise of promotion, which after 7 years on the job has been realized. In 1999, I started the job at $34,000/yr. which over seven years has increased to $63,000/yr.

To: Whom It May Concern,

In August of 1997 I gave birth to
being born with a serve handicap
twins again only loosing my son
very poor diagonoise. At 17 h
She had to have her spinal c
her spinal cord did not deve
would only live for a short
surgery (2nd surgery) they
brain, at 13 days old I was
brought her home for the fi
brain surgery due to shunt
surgery again. (4th surgery
down her chest and to her
(5th surgery) In Decembe
Hospital for yet another en
Hrydriphyllis (6th surgery
shunt replacement (brain s
down with a fever of 104.
day trying to get here feve
her Kidneys and Bladder
Infection). Come April o
underwent brain surgery
June and July
had to start catherizing he
learn how to catherize her
January 6th of 2000
of her shunt, the surgery
brain(we almost lost her)
with a complete shunt rep
fought the UTI. In June 2
revision. (11th surgery).
small intestines well the s
to repair her stomach and
52 f UTI and many stay
osed off her shunt so she had to have emergency brain surgery having a complete
new section of her brain.(13th surgery). The day
ded shunt revision

Dear Eastern Savings Bank,

Due to the untimely death of our daughter Jill and I were in a very stressful financial situation. This is due to the large medical bills resulting from our daughter's brain cancer. The time and stress of dealing with the illness had caused us to turn down business for our company. Since our daughter has passed away Jill and I can now devote more time to increasing the revenue from the business by getting new clients. We will be vigorously pursuing new clients and jobs to keep the company profitable and regain our financial freedom. If we are unable to get the revenue up we are going to sell the home and cash out the equity and find a new home. This plan was developed by bo of us with the help of American Mortgage, Inc.

Sincerely,

Robert Postman

Robert Postman

:00 FAX 757 499 7154
12:17P   L   , Comme

Going back to 1996, we went in and out of foreclosure problems almost immediately, as we were living from paycheck to paycheck prior to my layoff. In 1999, even though I had been hired at Hines VA, I filed for bankruptcy to save the house, my children's schooling and our peace of mind. Due to the fact that we had been receiving much less income over the period from 1996 through 2002 (when I worked up to the salary that I ended with in 1996), we were overwhelmed with medical bills and daily living expenses. I filed again in 2000 and my wife filed once more in 2001. Every time we filed we got better at getting close to even but not quite close enough. Refinancing would remove the burden of Chapter 13. Neither my wife or I have ever had a drug or gambling problem and we have been on only one vacation since getting married in 1979. We were only able to get the nice house and the down payment for it through an inheritance received from my Dad's family. Recently we caught up and currently have no car payments.

We have had a history of struggling with the mortgage, at first due to our change of income and then due to constantly playing catch up along with the extra Chapter 13 payments. Refinancing would give us the fresh start we need and now that I'm reestablished in my field with a steady government job I'll be able to meet my obligations. I have never looked to get out of my debt – only to get it under control and paid. I have not been fighting for my house – I have been fighting for our home. Please give us a chance to show that we are a good risk and thank you so much for your consideration.

Sincerely,

~~James~~ es G. MacDougal

CONTINUES ↑

To Whom It May Concern:

This letter serves as my written explanation for the late payment of my mortgage in late 2004 and early 2005. I have also attached some legal correspondence to provide some evidence of my situation.

In 2003, I was briefly married. Joint residence lasted less than 30 days and sadly due to threats to my life and family the marriage ended very disastrously. I conceived a child on our honeymoon which greatly complicated the matter. I learned that the he had a frightful past and had lied dreadfully to me and my family. As such a person would, after the physical separation and the knowledge that I could not get the marriage annulled due to the child, he tried to use my desire to protect my professional reputation and the safety of my daughter to blackmail me into payments to in effect grant me the divorce and "sell" his daughter. From our initial marriage in July 2003, thru the birth of my child he continued his threats and attempts at financial gain. After the birth of my daughter (prematurely at 34 weeks in April 2004) he began strong threats to take her away and fight me. I had worked with an attorney from mid – 2004 to determine my rights and a manner to gain a divorce and custody of my daughter. He would agree to terms with me and then change them to attempt negotiation. His initial requests were for $500,000 or he would ruin my life on an ongoing basis via my daughter and children.

I finally reached a point in late 2004 that he verbally agreed to me that if I would give him a large amount of money he would sign the papers and terminate his rights to my daughter. At the time I had no assets except for my home, but knew I had a bonus coming in March 2005 and if I could get him to sign my life could peacefully and safely move forward. Once I paid this money, he once again changed his story and he asked for another $250,000. This time I documented all financial obligations and with my attorney, I was finally successful in an alimony amount of $87,500 over a 3 year period. If you read the correspondence from my attorney in her disdain for my agreement, but in the end – I have my daughter.

I did not have the money –except to not pay my mortgage. Once I received my bonus I paid my account to date. When the divorce settled in July 2005 I was required per the settlement to pay him $10,000 in August as well as attorney's fees. I was late once again late until I could catch up again.

My business sold in late 2005 and per the W-2's provided to you as evidence of the increase in my income and assets.

I appreciate you understanding of this terrible matter in my past and know that it is no reflection of my commitment to meet any obligation to you.

Regards,

Stacie R. Roberts (signature)

Stacie R. Rob____

to major in interior architecture which i__ __s offered at Indiana University. We had l__ __ere only seven miles from the Indiana bo__ __really good since it dropped the amount b__ __nd dollars for each of my two daughter's __ __I had recommended to many of my client__ __r child's tuition and even leaving somethi__ __ts I put away, were staggering at slightly l__ __d about to dive head first into the proverbi__ __m for the first year's tuition, and move to __

__at had incurred steady but moderate appreci__ __a lot of the homes were for sale and the val__ __equity and moved to a model that had been b__ __nd only ten minutes further to the office in __

__the old home my wife complained of a heada__ __ded to lie down. I continued to pack up with r__ __later I went to my wife who was resting on a__ __S____all sized tumor and full hysterectomy__

To Whom It May Concern:

Re: Credit History

It was told to me it takes five years to recover from a divorce. No one said anything about the pitfalls along the way. While on paper everything looks possible, I did not know child support would be irregular because it was lost between social security and the state of Minnesota. I knew college expenses would play a part in my and my children's lives, but I was unprepared for medical and court costs and the real expenses of college and living costs.

I have three daughters, Amber, Kay, and Rebecca, who were still in high school when I became separated from my husband Thomas. At that time of the separation, Thomas was receiving Workers' Compensation and working part time. I was working full time.

Thomas is an alcoholic and has a controlling behavior. Every day after work he would stop for drinks. It was not unusual for him to spend $300-400 a week on alcohol. I had to have him removed from the property because he threatened to kill one of my children and me.

I tell you this because my credit problems began in our marriage and continued over the past five years because many of the creditors I owe are from this marriage. While my pay was on a regular basis, his was not. When it came time for the child support payments, often they were months behind and instead of making all of the monthly bills, I had to pay the most urgent at the time.

It has been the most difficult knowing my children do not receive financial or emotional support from their father. He does not contribute to any of their medical, automotive, or education expenses. I am their main support and principle parent.

There has been an ankle surgery, dental work, and the need for eyeglasses. Most recently, my middle child, Kay, has been diagnosed with mental and medical conditions. She has appointments with three doctors and a support group. While my insurance covers the majority of the costs, the co-pays add up and she is required to take several prescriptions. She has also been admitted twice to a facility for observation after harming herself. Presently she attends college. During her senior year in high school, she had some problems at her job and charges were filed against her. Court costs and restitution were required as well as paying back a sum of money. Since she did not have a job, I helped her with the costs. This past year I paid her housing of $325.00 a month and continue to support her, as she has not been able to find a job due to her diagnosis.

In January of this year, there was a problem with my youngest daughter's tuition payment, so I had to help her out with $1,500 to keep her in college and prevent her college loans from becoming due.

My goal now is to refinance my home and with the proceeds pay the outstanding creditors and get my credit in order. Since 2002, I have worked an additional job and completed the requirements for my master's degree. I have contributed regularly to an annuity and will continue to do so. I also plan to place a year's mortgage payments in an account so my payments are current. There are some improvements and upgrades required on the house as well. I would like to do those too.

However, if I am given this refinance, my main goal is to begin a credit history for myself.

Sincerely,

Jane D. Campbell
7 Bunker Hill Court
Maple Lake, MN 55358

I'm not a bad person because I have unsatisfactory credit, I'm a person that really wants to fix my situation, but had some unfortunate events that I have worked through.

so much for taking ... just listen and ... it. Giving me this ... help me fix my life ...

To Torcey Petterson

I **Doris Bardo** got behind on my mortgage payments to AUSA when my son became addicted to Myth and stole and forged checks on my account, stole my Father's guns that he left to me, his wife left him with no job and three children. My role in this was to pay checks off or put him in jail, I took in his wife and three kids, help her get trained for a job that they could live on without relying on me and get her into a place to live. I also got managed to get my son into a methadone clinic in southeast. This all set me back a lot without the help of my daughter I would have never made it. The result of all of this plus getting my guns back kept me behind with residual Of debt which I can't seem to get the back payment made up totally. I have All the guns back, my ex-daughter in law and kids a place to live and On their own and she finished her associates in accounting. This and the thrill of my son out clean and a job working as a mechanic again, and also paying his child support, not asking me for money and even acknowledging that he owes me money and will try to pay it back as soon as he gets past arrears of child support most likely two more years.

I rented the apartment down stairs but the tenants tore it up ruined carpet, knocked holes in walls, broke bath tube and tub surround with a hammer, tore up cupboard doors, broke window, left house full of furniture, and apt.

FORECLOSED!

continues on page 78!

Very dirty, with two carpets ruined. This all cost me $ 2846. I still have their furniture in storage for 8 more months before I can dispose of it. The apt. is all back to normal and I have my daughter living their and as of 5-1-2006 will be receiving rent of the Apt, again. I have tried to serve the evicted tenants with small claims case but their not to be found. I feel that I can make this Mortgage payment because Apartment is rented, I'm no longer helping my ex- daughter in law; my son is clean and on his Own and not needing my help and he also knows I done all for him I can do there is a firm understanding if he mess up he is on his own. I know the Mortgage payment will be larger but it will also include the second mortgage payment and I will not be paying the late payment fees. It will also help that I have a income from the apt now, as my daughter is in their and has always had a very healthy relationship with me and carries her own weight and has helped me also. I have $900 from rent, 1511 from VA and Wages which was if I member right was 56,000 last year. I want the Mortgage payment taken out of the bank on the 3 rd of each month. The extra money I have ask for I plan to pay the rest of the money I owe On the repair of the basement apt. and to pay of what is left on my credit card. I sorry for getting behind but at the time I seen no other way and With your help I can get back on time and not worry every minute.

Thank You
Doris Bardo 5-22-06

55

this photo FOUND by Sarah Arteaga, Conway, AR

November 20, 1968

Dear 'TEENer:

The joke's on us!

Were we ever surprised to get all of your letters requesting the Braille Booklet advertised in Underground Christmas!

Why?

Because that ad was not a real ad, but a joke ad (thus no department number). HINT: That's how you tell the true from the false--the real ads ALWAYS have department numbers.

But we just couldn't let you down...so all of us here at 'TEEN put our heads together and came up with the attached Braille Guide. A booklet it's not---but if you study it for awhile, you'll be able to write hundreds of slang expressions of your very own--in Braille!

Thanks for your interest. Happy holidays to ya!

Sincerely,

THE 'TEEN STAFF

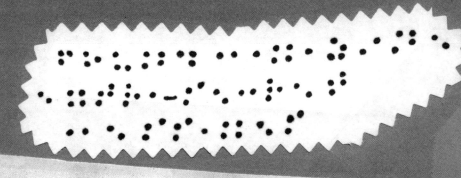

HERE IT IS!

YOUR GROOVY TEEN SLANG GUIDE--IN BRAILLE!

We're giving you the Braille spelling for some current "IN" expressions, then you can study our Braille alphabet and write hundreds and hundreds of your very OWN slang expressions.

In Braille, the dots representing each letter are raised slightly so that the blind person can "read" by feel. If you want to raise these dots, just press them gently on the back side of the paper with a sharp pencil.

Raised or not, the Braille slang guide/ alphabet gives you a great new code. You can write extra-secret messages... make outasite posters and signs... be very, very IN!

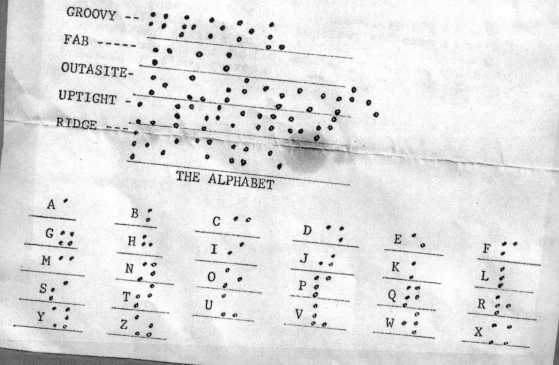

GROOVY --

FAB -----

OUTASITE-

UPTIGHT -

RIDGE ---

THE ALPHABET

Davy drops the beat...

I grew up reading Daniel Clowes' devilishly funny and engrossing *Eightball* comics, and the movie *Ghost World*—which he adapted from his own comics—is one of my all-time favorites. Turns out, Dan's also a world-class collector of Found stuff. Over the next eight pages, he shares some prized finds and the strange stories behind them.

Davy: How long have you been collecting finds?

Dan: I've been picking up Found stuff ever since I can remember. But I think I started saving them when I lived in Chicago, so most of my collection is from Chicago and the East Bay.

Davy: Okay, let's start with *Imemyselfism*. This was left on your car?

Dan: Yeah, it was this guy Master Watkins. He was a really prolific pamphleteer on the South Side of Chicago in the mid-'80s. His flyers were always on different colored paper. This was one from maybe 1984.

Davy: Were they all the same type of thing—asking for money?

Dan: Yeah, send him money and he'll give you some spiritual guidance. The specifics are never outlined in the flyers; it's just vague and cryptic enough to hook you.

Davy: You never sent in cash to get all the details?

Dan: No, but believe me, I was tempted.

Davy: It would almost be worth it.

GHOSTSHRIMP.

"IMEMYSELFISM"

1. GREATEST LIVING RELIGION ON EARTH!; ONE WHICH TEACHES MAN TO THINK FOR HIMSELF, AND, NOT GO BY WHAT OTHERS (WHO ARE (PROBABLY LESS INTELLIGENT THAN YOU) SAY!

2. IMEMYSELFISM IS JUST WHAT THE LETTERS SPELL OUT, NO MYSTERY; WE AIN'T GOT A LOT OF TIME TO WASTE ON STUPID THINGS. WE DON'T HAVE ANY OF OUR PRECIOUS, AND, VITAL TIME TO SPEND TALK-ING ABOUT THE OTHER MAN, WOMAN, OR, CHILD — WE ONLY DEAL WITH FACTS. AND, UNLESS YOU ARE COMPLETELY SINCERE, IMEMYSELFISM HAS NO PLACE FOR YOU.

3. THERE IS NO GREATER SOURCE OF KNOWLEDGE THAN IMEMYSELFISM, ALL OTHER BELIEFS PALE IN COMPARISON — HAPPINESS, WEALTH, PEACE OF MIND, ETC., ARE ALL SECOND NATURE TO US — WE ARE THE GREATEST OF THEM ALL!!

DO YOU KNOW WHO GOD IS? WELL, THE BEST ANSWERS ARE FOUND WITH IMEMYSELFISM!!

SEND $25 TO $50 OFFERING TO:

IMEMYSELFISM
JOSEPH WATKINS (MASTER)
P. O. Box 157578
Chicago, IL 60615

YOUR ANSWER SHEET WILL COME! DON'T FORGET YOUR NAME, ADDRESS AND PHONE — PLEASE PRINT!

CONTINUED ON NEXT PAGE →

Dan: I think about it now and I'm like, 'Why didn't I do it?' I guess the thought of twenty-five bucks back then was a mountain of dough. I was like, 'Twenty-five bucks? Where'm I gonna get twenty-five bucks?' You know?

Davy: Yeah, exactly! But I wonder if this scheme worked for him? I mean, if he kept putting these pamphlets everywhere he must've been doing all right with it.

Dan: Well, for like six months I would see his pamphlets all over the place—on the windshields of cars, tucked in apartment doors and mailboxes. He was ninja-like—everyone in the neighborhood got these flyers but no one knew who he was or ever glimpsed him leaving them around. I'd get home at three or four in the morning and when I woke up around noon, there'd be a new one on my car. It was a riddle of sorts.

Davy: I always prefer my spiritual gurus to have an air of mystery.

Dan: Now that I think of it, if I'd really wanted to, I could've just gone to the copy shop—they must have known who he was! And now it's too late. I don't think Joseph Watkins would be an easy name to Google.

Davy: We can try 'Master Watkins.'

Dan: Yeah! The flyers went on for about six months and then Master Watkins suddenly vanished.

CONTINUED FROM PREVIOUS PAGE!

Davy: Okay, what's up with this find: *Anna, I like you for a girl friend and I wint you to go swimg tomoroy, but I mit not be—*

Dan: *—Beabel to come!*

Davy: And you are pretty anna and I wont you to come to the tree house at eight oclock at night I will be there. By Mark Bunce.

Dan: Okay, so my Grandma had this little house in Western Michigan. Me and my cousins would go there every year. And that was a note found by my cousin Anna; it was presumably written to her by the sub-literate next-door neighbor. Anna was probably eleven years-old and the boy was like fifteen. He was not the brightest, but he sure was persistent.

Davy: So what was her response?

Dan: To run in terror! The appropriate response, I think.

Davy: But if you don't know the story it seems very sweet.

Dan: The note was found a second time—by me—twenty years later. I was about thirteen when the note was written, but I'd had the foresight to stash it in one of my school notebooks. It had become sort of a famous thing in my family. Me and my cousins always quoted it—instead of saying, "Hey, you wanna go swimming," we would say "Hey, wanna go swimg?" The note became the source of an entire private language we had. Strangely, when I found it again, I discovered that there was a lot of stuff we'd made up—stuff I thought had been in the note that wasn't actually there. We thought it was much more perverted than it actually was.

When you have questions I deliver answers

CLAIRVOYANT READINGS

WITH
REV. ROSS URRERE

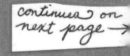

continued on next page →

Hello:

I have been doing readings and healing for about nine years now. I have been trained by some of the best and I continue to take classes to refine my technique. I have worked with hundreds of people from all walks of life. I have always felt privileged that they have come into my life that I might practice my trade. It allows me to be a continual student of life and see a reflection of myself in others.

I have had many different experiences and opportunities in life that I can draw upon while working with a client. Currently I am involved with the production of a series of videos dealing in the correct use of psychic power. I have been a staff member of the Academy of Psychic Studies for over 6 years. I have served in our countries armed forces, worked with a major rock & roll promoter, been stage crew for a ballet company, owned and operated a hot glass studio and have dealt with all the different aspects of the Arts.

I ride motorcycles every day, deal with computers and video equipment and I enjoy working with people. I have fallen in and out of love, felt like I was on the mountain top and then walked through some valleys. Last, but not least, I can still laugh at my creations and am convinced that I have had a lot of help along the way from the Supreme Being acting through the people in my life.

I offer a variety of Clairvoyant Readings including:
Aura Readings • Relationship Readings • Psychic Physicals (Ask me about this one!) • Male Reality Checks • Career Readings
$20.00 for a half -hour session and $45.00 for a full 1½ reading.

When you need answers to your questions......Call (510) 549-1991 for an appointme 1.

THIS IS A UNIVERSAL MESSAGE

FOR ALL PEOPLE THAT WANT TO DO RIGHT

Brothers don't ever put your penis, in your woman's mouth because this spoils your woman. When you put your penis, in your woman's mouth or in her rectum, you are misusing your woman, And what you are doing to her is: you are starting your woman out on A Sexual Habit. And you are not conscious of what you are doing to her.

This is what causes all of our young peoples marriages to go sour. This is the reason that all of our young people start fussing and fighting like cats and dogs six months to A year after their marriage.

Now, the reason that all of our young people's marriage start messing up in about 3 to 6 months is because, it takes about 3 to 6 months before that mess, that you shoots in her mouth, begins to take an affect on her brain.

Now, it mess you up to, but, it messes your woman up Quicker then it mess you up, because she's got the thing in her mouth, and she gets the full load every time, and you are licking a hole, so you are missing most of yours, so that's why it messes her up Quicker then it mess you up.

And the affects that this mess have on your woman is: it clogs up the love current in her brain, and she don't have any feelings for you any more. And the more of this mess she eats the less feelings she have for you.

And it works the same way on you, as it works on her. You see, when you eat this mess, It makes you hard headed, and rebellius, and cold blooded, It kills the love in you, It makes you selfish, and small minded, and you can't reason with your woman any more, because all she can think of is, sex sex sex, just like A sissy. And, that's why all the arguements start.

If that young man knew, that when he starts putting his penis, in his woman's mouth that, that was the begining of the end, of his love affair, he would chop off his right arm, before he would ask her to do that to him. But he is not conscious of what he is doing to her, if he loves her.

And when after he messes her up, they finally come to the conclusion, that Love don't last. But, that's a LIE. LOVE DO LAST. Love will last you A LIFETIME, IF you don't misuse it. And when you put your penis, in your woman's mouth, or in her rectum. you are mis-use-ing your Love. And that's why it turns sour on you. So don't mis-use your woman, And she will Love you for the rest of your Life.

If you and your woman have this problem. NOW. What you have to do is that you and your woman will have to get your heads together, and KICK, YOUR SEXUAL HABIT, And once you have Kicked, Your Sexual Habit, You can get your Love Life back together again.

COURTESY OF THE RIGHTEOUS

FINDER'S SPOTLIGHT: DANIEL CLOWES

CONTINUED

Davy: It swelled in your imaginations?

Dan: Yeah, and we imagined into it what he was really thinking.

Davy: I love how you always end up quoting Found notes back and forth with your friends like lines from your favorite movies. Me and my friends do that, too.

Dan: Even my wife—I met her twenty years later, and told her the story of this note, and I don't think she and I have ever actually said the word 'swimming.' We always say '*swimg.*' Even with my son, we say, 'Hey, do you want to go *swimg?*'

Davy: So your son, he might be at school asking his friends, 'Want to go swimg?' I like the power of this Found note, that it became this family lore. Some of the strangest terms and phrases in Found notes stick with you. Like this note someone found in Chicago, it said "Dear Irma, Can I have *at least* five dollars? If not can I have two ciggterts?" So my friend in Chicago, he only says 'ciggterts!' He'll be like, "Yo, I'm going to the store, anybody need ciggterts?"

Dan: Exactly—it becomes such second nature, you just say it without any inflection. You know, I haven't really spoken to either of my cousins in about ten years or so. I wonder if they'd remember that note. That would be funny to ask them.

Davy: Your cousin Anna is probably shacking up with Mark Bunce right now!

Dan: Man, I wonder where Mark Bunce is these days.

Davy: Maybe he knows about Imemyselfism. And became Master Bunce?

Dan: Undoubtedly!

I GOT SO MUCH WORK TO DO
I CANT STOP NOW
I TOOK A BREAK FROM MUSIC
NIGGAS had WRITTEN ME OUT
SO IM COMING BACK STRONG
MONEY STAYS LONG
NIGGAS SAY IM WRONG
UNTIL THEY SEE MY BITCH IN HER THONG
AND ALL DAY LONG THEY BREAK IN PAPER
WHILE I PULL THEM CAPERS
FRONTIN LIKE SOME PLAYAS
WHILE YOU TALKIN LIKE A HATA
ILL SEE ya LATA I GOT SOME WORK TO DO
LIKE I SAID BEFORE
AINT NO BLUFFIN OR NO PERPIN DUDE
CELLY ALWAYS CHIRPIN
ATTITUDE ON RUDE
MEAN MUG ON MY FACE
BLOOD ON MY NIKE SHOES
I PAID MY DUES
SO BACK UP DUDE
BEFORE you GET YOUR GRILL DISMANTLE
IM FEELIN' HY PHY AS FUCK
CATCH ME ON THE HUSTLE CHANNEL
NIGGAS ASKIN BOUT KD
IM GOIN TO GIVE EM A SAMPLE
DROP THE BEAT AND WATCH IT SMOKE LIKE CAMEL

CONTINUED ON NEXT PAGE →

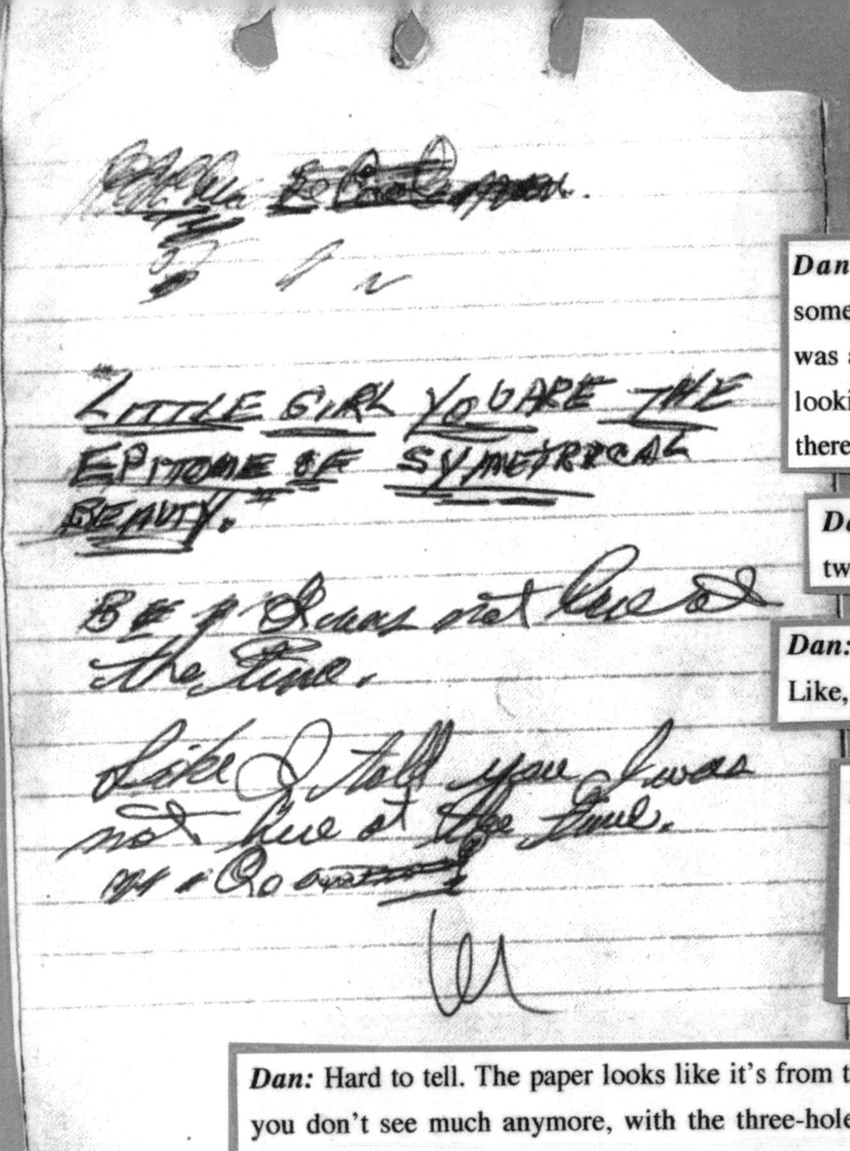
LITTLE GIRL YOU ARE THE EPITOME OF SYMMETRICAL BEAUTY.

Like I tell you I was not here at the time.

Davy: What about this one: *Little girl you are the epitome of symmetrical beauty*. You found it in a desk drawer?

Dan: Yeah, that's a great one. I think we wer somewhere on location making *Ghost World*. The was an old desk in the corner and I rifled through i looking for just this sort of stuff. That note was i there and I was like, 'I'm taking this! It's mine now.'

Davy: It looks like the text was written ove twice, once with a pencil and once with a pen.

Dan: Right, like he was really working on that li Like, *I'm gonna use this and it's gonna play tonight!*

Davy: Yeah, and there's something slightly creepy about the use of 'Little girl.' I mean, maybe he's a sixty year-old talking to a fifty year-old? Or maybe it's something more Mark Bunce-like?

Dan: Hard to tell. The paper looks like it's from the '50s. Sort of yellowed. It's from a pad tha you don't see much anymore, with the three-hole thing at the top. My speculation: He was a security guard. And maybe during those mind-numbing hours of the night he was sitting at hi security desk writing song lyrics or a love note or whatever.

CONTINUED FROM PREVIOUS PAGES!

Davy: Yeah, but it's weird how it says below, *I was not here at the time—like I told you I was not here at the time.*

Dan: Who can ever know the story behind it?

Davy: And then there's this one: *THIS IS A UNIVERSAL MESSAGE FOR ALL THE PEOPLE THAT WANT TO DO RIGHT. Brothers don't ever put your penis in your woman's mouth….*

Dan: That one! It was in the streets of Chicago. At first I thought it was just some kind of advertisement and I almost threw it away, but then I started reading and was like, 'Holy God!'

Davy: I think it's absolutely amazing.

Dan: Yeah, when you first look at it, it has this vibe like, 'This is gonna be some kind of really long, boring, probably religious nonsense that I don't want to read,' but then you see the word '*rectum*' and it's like, *Wow!*

Davy: It's funny because after I read this I did some online research and strangely I couldn't find anything to support the premise.

Dan: Yeah, the scientific basis for this is elusive at best. Thank God I found this flyer or I would've never learned this stuff.

Davy: You've got a ton of other fantastic finds here. Like these rap lyrics.

Dan: I found them years ago while walking through Piedmont, California, one of the richest and whitest communities in Northern California.

Davy: Naturally! So, could I ask you to talk more generally about your attraction to Found things?

anna I like you for a girl feirnd and I wint you to go swing tomoroy but I mit not beabel to come and you are pretty anna and I wont you to come to the tree house at 8,00 oclock at nitght I will be there

by mark Bunce

and gerve me a kiss

Dan: I think it's just seeing that human quality. Everything we typically encounter has been processed by so many human hands. And it's been sharpened so carefully to impart a certain kind of message. So to see something like *Imemyselfism*—guys selling their weird religion—or 'Don't abuse your woman's mouth'—it's just so personal and unfiltered and real. Like those angry notes you get on your car. When I see a note like that, I always just go and steal it! *'Next time take up three spaces, asshole!'* In a sanitized world, you don't really get to see that real, intense anger too much anymore.

Davy: Yeah, I like how Found notes contain a kind of emotional nakedness.

Dan: This weird thing happened recently. I came out to my car one morning and someone had stuck something under my windshield wiper—it turned out to be a newspaper clipping about this comic convention that I was making an appearance at. I thought, 'Oh, one of my neighbors saw an article about me and left it for me,' and then I unfolded it and inside someone had written, *'YOU'RE BLOCKING MY DRIVEWAY, FUCKHEAD!'* It was just totally random that they'd used a page from *The San Francisco Chronicle* with an article about me to write me a nasty note. I kind of loved the serendipity of it.

Davy: Do you continue to pick stuff up?

Daniel Clowes' books are available from Fantagraphics Books.

Checkity-check 'em out!

Dan: Oh yeah! My wife and I walk with our heads down all the time. And we can't help but pick up every soggy piece of paper we see on the sidewalk. Our son is four, and he hasn't gotten into it yet. But we'll definitely teach him how to find the goods. That's one great thing about Found stuff: It's always being made.

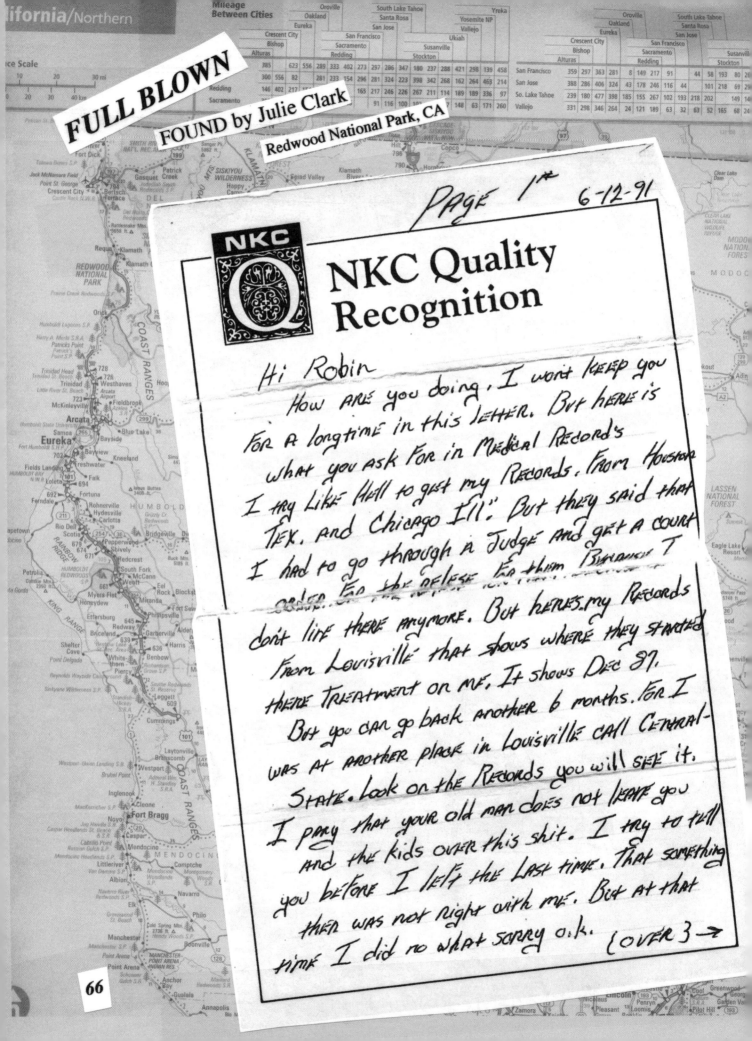

PAGE 1ˢᵗ   6-12-91

NKC Quality Recognition

Hi Robin

How ARE you doing, I won't KEEP you
For A longtime in this letter. But here is
what you ask For in Medical Record's
I try Like Hell to get my Records. From Houston
TEX. and Chicago Ill." But they said that
I had to go through A Judge and get A court
order For the release For them. Because I
don't live there anymore. But here's my Records
From Louisville that shows where they started
there TREATMENT on ME. It shows Dec 87.
But you can go back another 6 months. For I
was at another place in Louisville call Central-
State. Look on the Records you will see it.
I pray that your old man does not leave you
and the kids over this shit. I try to tell
you before I left the Last time. That something
then was not right with me. But at that
time I did no what sorry o.k.   [OVER 3 →

66

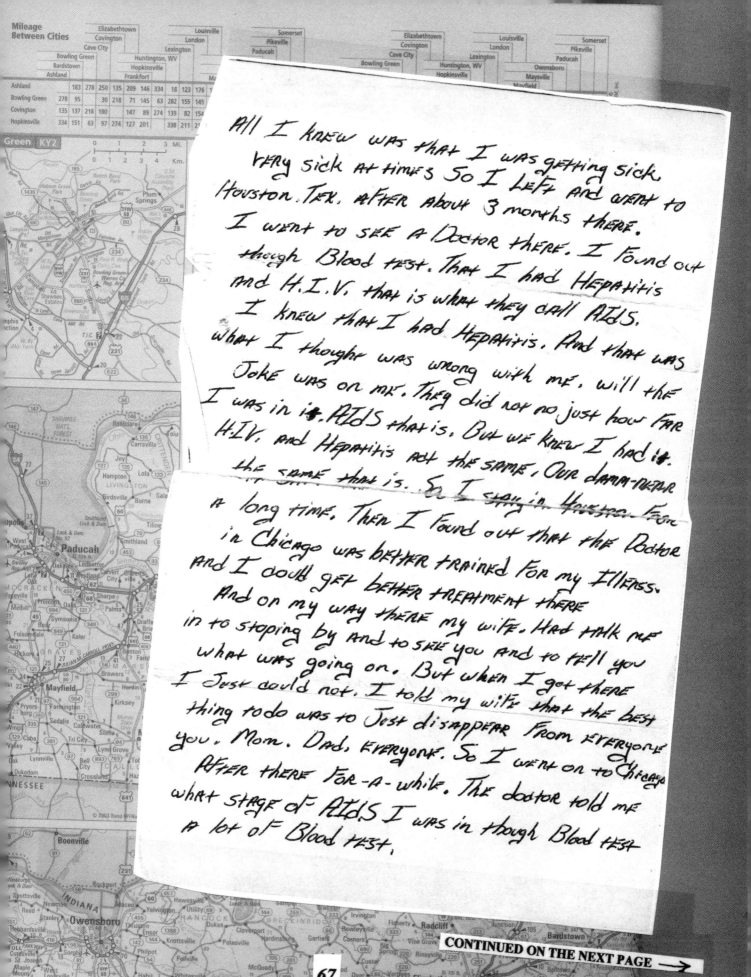

All I knew was that I was getting sick. Very sick at times. So I left and went to Houston. Tex. After about 3 months there. I went to see a Doctor there. I found out though Blood test. That I had Hepatitis and H.I.V. that is what they call AIDS. I knew that I had Hepatitis. And that was what I thought was wrong with me. will the joke was on me. They did not no just how far I was in it. AIDS that is. But we knew I had it. H.I.V. and Hepatitis act the same, Our damm-near the same that is. So I stay in Houston for a long time. Then I found out that the Doctor in Chicago was better traind for my illens. And I could get better treatment there. And on my way there my wife. Had talk me in to stoping by and to see you and to tell you what was going on. But when I got there I Just could not. I told my wife that the best thing to do was to Just disappear from everyone you. Mom. Dad, everyone. So I went on to Chicago. After there for-a-while. The doctor told me what stage of AIDS I was in though Blood test. A lot of Blood test,

CONTINUED ON THE NEXT PAGE →

NKC Quality Recognition

There are 3 stages of H.I.V.

1st one is a carried a person that can have it. And carried it to other people.

2nd two - is A.R.K. that is symptoms of H.I.V. And 3rd three - The "Bitch" is what I call it. But they call it Full Blown A.I.D.S. I was in A-R-K- I carried the symptoms of Full Blown - But by my Blood work they could tell that I had some time left. Before. I went to FullBlown. It were just take time Before I were to get there. The Doctor said. He was right. I try to tell you. I call From Chicago. If you remember. At that time you said you was getting married and decided not to tell you. At that time no one knew. But me my wife. And Doctors. It was For the best.

(OVER) →

You DESERVE A NEW START in Life. And I
had it in my mind NOT to Fuck-it-up. For you.
So I had my NAME change. And to make
SURE no one knew who I was. Tell the time
got Right. As of 1990 I have went to
Full-Blown-A.I.D.S. now. I have to take
more medicing. A.Z.T. and more shit to.
I am in to Chenotherapy. it is For a Form
of CANCER. WE call it k.S.! Now to you
I don't no why you are so piss-off. You got
what you wanted the kid or kids
For you said and you said it more then ones
That you could NEVER have me For every
But you wanted my and yours Kids I gave you
that. One thing that I NEVER gave to another women
I pray every day that it does not show up
in you H.I.V. that is. I would not wish that
on my worse Ememy. H.I.V. Is a very horrible
way to die. But you say you would love
to no when I do die From it. Will I have
made sure though my people that you will no.
So you can have a drink and have a panty
But you should come and watch them

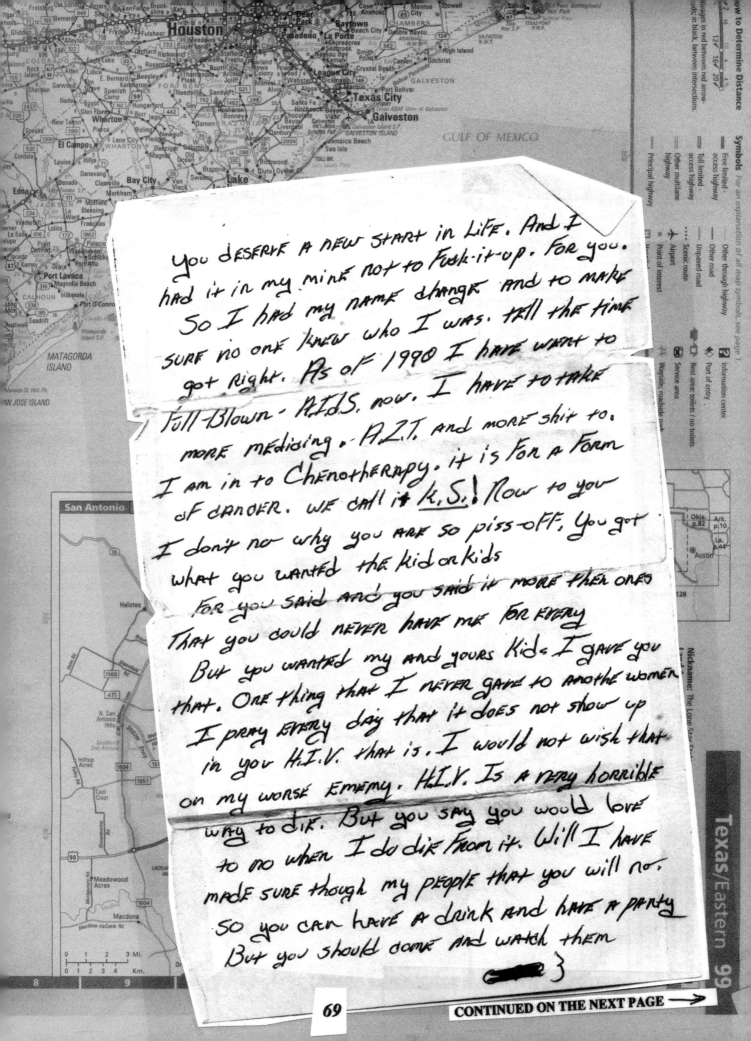

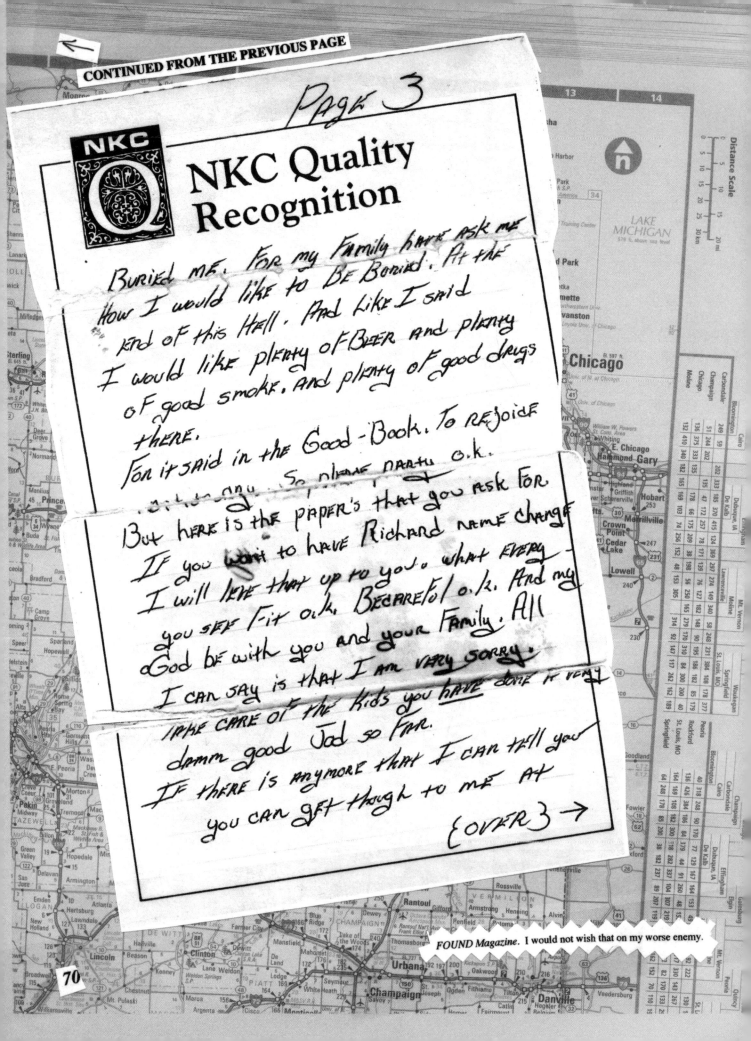

PAGE 3

NKC Quality Recognition

Buried me. For my Family have ask me
How I would like to Be Buried. At the
end of this Hell. And Like I said
I would like plenty of Beer and plenty
of good smoke. and plenty of good drugs
there.
For it said in the Good-Book. To Rejoice
... So please party o.k.

But here is the paper's that you ask for
If you want to have Richard name change
I will leve that up to you. what ever
you see Fit o.k. Becareful o.k. And my
God be with you and your Family. All
I can say is that I am very sorry.
Take care of the kids you have done it very
damm good Jod so Far.
If there is anymore that I can tell you
you can get though to me At

[OVER] →

FOUND Magazine. I would not wish that on my worse enemy.

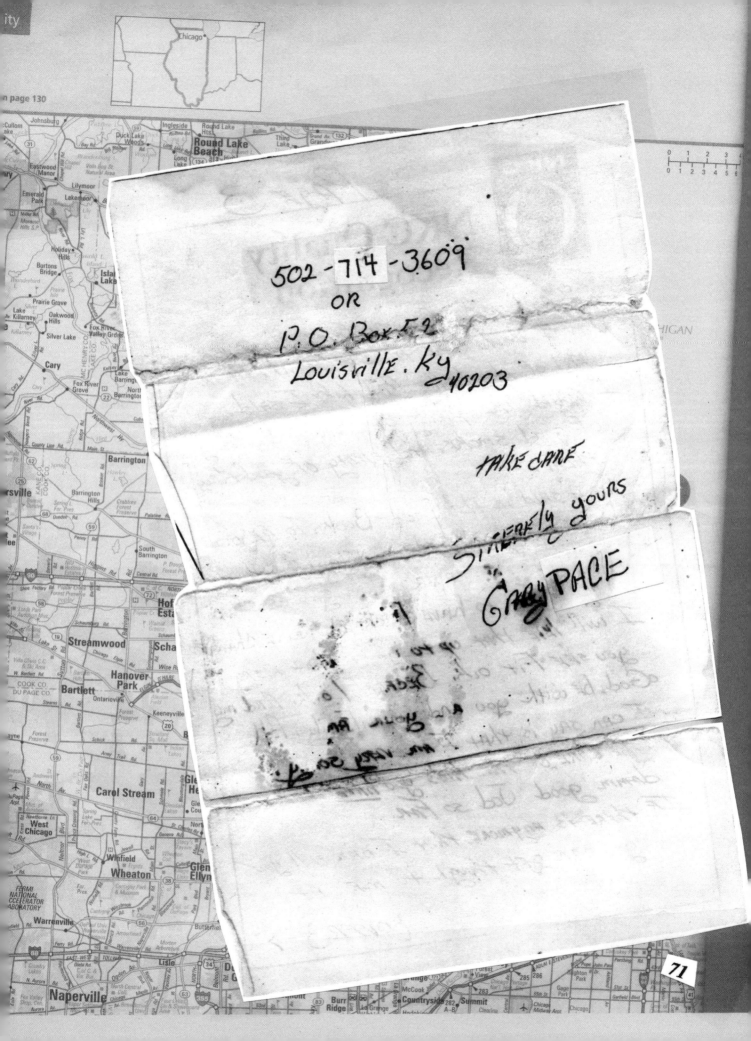

502-714-3609
OR
P.O. Box 52
Louisville, Ky 40203

TAKE CARE

SINCERELY YOURS

GARY PACE

71

To our Four Fingered Friend

FOUND GLOVE

SPECIALLY FITTED FOR PERSONS HAVING ONLY FOUR FINGERS

RIGHT HAND

GLOVE IS ORANGE WITH MULTI-PURPOSE GRIP MESH

YOUR 4 DIGIT HAND CAN BE WARM AGAIN

DO NOT WORRY!!!!!

GLOVE HAS BEEN OUT OF HARM'S WAY SINCE SUNDAY, FEBRUARY 17, 2008 AT 2:07 PM

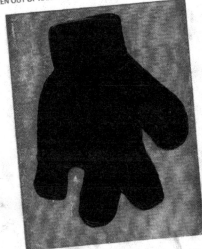

If this GLOVE has been made for your special hand, please call:

Brittany @ (602) 738-1486.

TO OUR FOUR FINGERED FRIEND

FOUND by Faith Purvis   Flagstaff, AZ

BUBBLE-MAKER-WAND

FOUND by Brock Hanson

San Francisco, CA

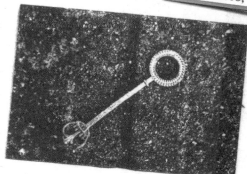

A Lost bubble-maker-wand

FOUND

no ~~reward~~ reward necc-essary. pls. email: LOstANDFoUND.PIECE@gmail.com and we'll return to you A.S.A.P.

WANTEd - TWO WHITE CAUCASIAN MEN WITH CALIFORNIA ID OR MILITARY ID
TO go to Shooting RANGE IN SF SAN FRANCISCO
Required to shoot ONE RouNd
FoR $3000 FoR EACH GUY
I WILL RENT GUN
CALL JAMES
415-567-7497

TWO WHITE CAUCASIAN MEN

FOUND by Däg

San Francisco, CA

MISSING CAT

Bishop Alvarez, a Russian Blue (all grey) cat, was last seen at the side of the road unconscious or **DEAD** on August 25th, at 8:00 pm, in front of 3055 W. Logan Blvd. His owner was notified immediately, and within minutes (two to be exact) went to retrieve Bishop so that a proper burial could be held. To his surprise, Bishop was gone. Please, if you know anything about how Bishop died, or where his body was disposed of, contact his family immediately. We miss him so much and need closure.

Max & Heather
(773)459-5
(847)729-

Note: Bishop had surgery a couple of years ago to remove his penis due to severe crystals blocking his urinary tract, so he could have been mistaken for a female cat.

TWO TO BE EXACT

REWARD!!!!
LOST DOG!!!!

Name is "BRADY". Wriggled out of Collar on Par thenon Avenue. Last seen on Long Blvd near 31st Avenue.

He is basically scared of his own shadow and is very nice. He is my girlfriend's dog and I will never get laid again unless I find him! I will give a reward of $100 to anyone that helps me find him! Call 615-668-09___ if you see him!

BRADY

FOUND by Paige Smithson Nashville, TN

LOST
1 SHOE

Looks like this

CALL CODY
416-255-4___

LOOKS LIKE THIS

FOUND by Anita Corsini Toronto, ON

24 HOUR SCIENCE FRIEND

FOUND by Sara Watson Chicago, IL

SCIENCE FRIEND WANTED!

questions answered to

I love science but my friends don't. I like to talk about any type of science or technology: computers (hardware and software), biology, chemistry, electronic music, botany, medical, etc. Astronomy is my favorite. If you have stuff you'd like to discuss, you can call me 24 hr. Tell the answering machine why you are calling and I will answer if I'm home. Personal stuff is ok too but there are 5 subjects that I will not discuss: sports, religion, politics, sex, or history (except science related). Phone is off the hook when I'm not available.

Science Fri 24 hrs (773)225-0

Science Fr 24 hrs (773)325-0

Science F 24 hrs (773)325-0

Science F 24 hrs (773)325-0

Science Fr 24 hrs (773)325-

Science 24 hrs (773)325-

Science 24 hour (773)325-

MY DAD

FOUND by Byron Case

Cotton Correctional Facility
Cameron, MO

my Dad

John Allen Cenovich

(Jack) boyhood name

16 September 2008

Dear Davy,

Prison is not an ideal place to find things. Inmates tend to hold tightly to what precious few belongings they're permitted and, when the time comes to rid oneself of some of those things, they generally do so under a tight veil of secrecy. Notes get shredded into a hundred pieces and flushed down the toilet, photos are slipped between the pages of magazines and flushed down the through the property room, old letters are burned, and so on. That I should find that most precious of all belongings, a photograph, snugly wedged into the pages of Steinbeck's The Pearl last week was incredible.

I've studied this partial image for a while. There is an ephemeral haunting quality to it that I do not see every time I look at it. One moment I just see a working-class tabletop setting — the spread newspaper, a box of Price Saver white facial tissue, a large reference book of some kind, a few business cards and receipts on the windowsill — but after a period I pick up on the balance of light and dark, and on the presence of people in the absence of faces. The latter is something I have always found mildly disturbing, and that the picture looks like it was taken in a near-black room with a too-bright flash setting doesn't help any. Outside the window, if you look closely, there appear to be densely interwoven tree branches, all devoid of foliage. In a nutshell, the whole thing has kind of an eerie "Blair Witch" aura and I don't much care for it. Consider it property of FOUND.

Best wishes,

Byron
Byron

Dear Found,
    I am an inmate at the Eastern Oregon Correction
institution. I recently got a chance to view one of your ma
in fact it was issue #3 from Feb. 2004. I really enjoy
it, and was happy to see that you often grant prisoner's
request for free issues, I myself would like to know if yo
would please send me one. I saw in the issue I read that
were, at that time, planning to rele

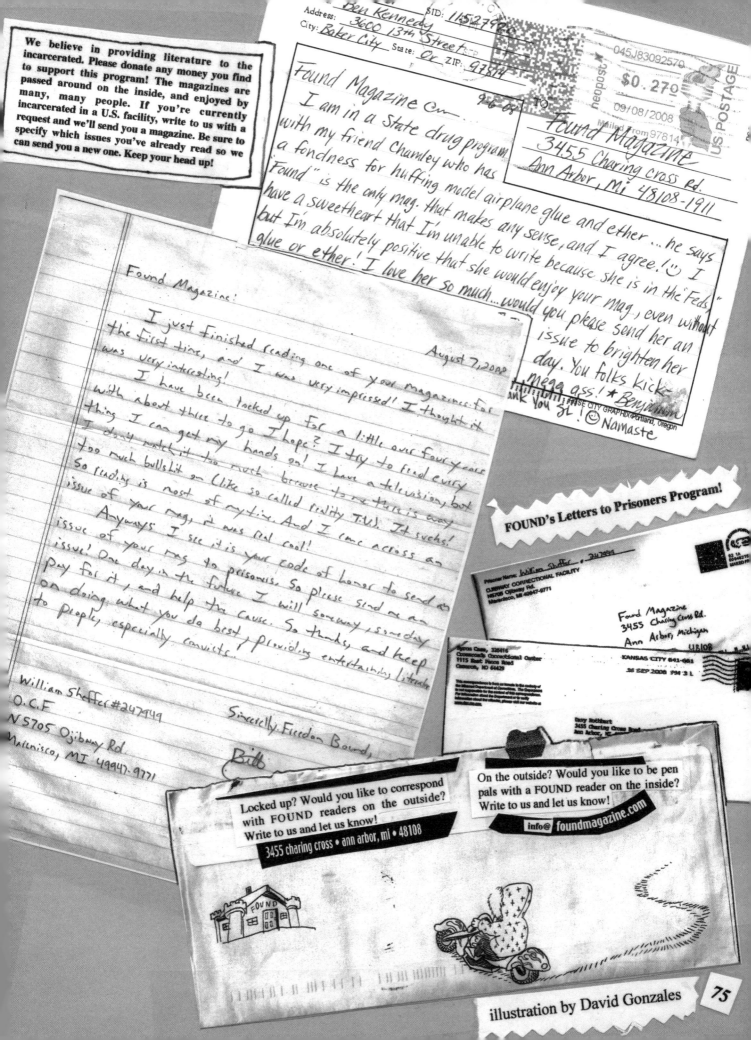

Address: Ben Kennedy
3600 13th Street
City: Baker City   State: Or   ZIP: 97814

SID: 1152792

045J83092570
$0.270
09/08/2008

TO
Found Magazine
3455 Charing Cross Rd.
Ann Arbor, MI 48108-1911

Found Magazine —
9-6-08

I am in a State drug program, with my friend Chamley who has a fondness for huffing model airplane glue and ether... he says "Found" is the only mag. that makes any sense, and I agree! (☺) I have a sweetheart that I'm unable to write because she is in the "Feds," but I'm absolutely positive that she would enjoy your mag., even without glue or ether! I love her so much... would you please send her an issue to brighten her day. You folks kick mega ass! ✱ Benjamin

thank you SL! ☺ Namaste

FIRSE CITY GRAPHIX Portland, Oregon

Found Magazine!

August 7, 2008

I just finished reading one of your magazines for the first time, and I was very impressed! I thought it was very interesting!

I have been locked up for a little over four years with about three to go I hope? I try to read every thing I can get my hands on! I have a television, but I don't watch it too much because to me tv is way too much bullshit on (like so called reality T.V.). It sucks! So reading is most of my time. And I came across an issue of your mag. it was real cool!

Anyways! I see it is your code of honor to send an issue of your mag. to prisoners. So please send me an issue! One day in the future I will someway, someday pay for it, and help the cause. So thanks, and keep on doing what you do best, providing entertaining literature to people, especially convicts.

Sincerely, Freedom Bound,

William Shaffer #247949
O.C.F
N 5705 Ojibway Rd.
Manisco, MI 49947-9771

Bill

Prisoner Name: William Shaffer • 247949
OJIBWAY CORRECTIONAL FACILITY
N5705 Ojibway Rd.
Manisco, MI 49947-9771

Found Magazine
3455 Charing Cross Rd.
Ann Arbor, Michigan
48108

KANSAS CITY 641-661
16 SEP 2008 PM 3 L

Byron Case, 320616
Crossroads Correctional Center
1115 East Pence Road
Cameron, MO 64429

Davy Rothbart
3455 Charing Cross Road
Ann Arbor, M...

Locked up? Would you like to correspond with FOUND readers on the outside? Write to us and let us know!

On the outside? Would you like to be pen pals with a FOUND reader on the inside? Write to us and let us know!

info@foundmagazine.com

3455 charing cross • ann arbor, mi • 48108

illustration by David Gonzales

FOUND by Kate Stryker

Austin, TX

2/22/00

Alyssa,

Six months later I am back at the Elephant Room for happy hour sitting at the bar writing you. It seems a little crazy that we are now engaged. Crazy, but beautiful. I don't remember exactly what I wrote last time, but I remember being quite enamored with you then and a little nervous that you might not be quite as head over heels as I was. Luckily it has all worked out. I do feel lucky that we finally found each other again and at the right time in our lives. I think you are perfect for me — allow me to rephrase — I know you are perfect for me & I can't wait to spend the rest of our lives together. Everything seems right about you, about us,

Not only do you make me happy, but you inspire me to be a better person & to live my life more fully. Being in love with you for the rest of my life is going to be amazingly beautiful.

I am off to tell Obama that he will need to do something about the cost of animal dental care. I love you.

CRAIG

FOUND Magazine. Crazy, but beautiful.

America's got talent

I love you more than Obama loves Hillary!

♡ heddes

BACK-HANDED VALENTINE

FOUND by Raphaela

Denver, CO

⑤ I care about you, scratch that, love you very much I only hope all my rambling can convey that message.

　　　Happy Valentine Day '07

→ that is, if you'll be my valentine you cutie patootie with the big fat bootie.

↳ Note: that was rennie!

P.S. Don't read too closely, I know my grammar and word choice isn't always that good and I know your a lil smartie pants with this stuff with your 690 on the SAT verbal and all. (I'm not competitive).

PATOOTIE WITH THE BIG FAT BOOTIE

FOUND by Meaghan Henry

San Francisco, CA

OMG, I just had a revelation, I really, really care about Eleni, I think its the atmosphere, it being V-day. OMG ELENI!

OMG Get a grip Man!

SHELF LIFE

FOUND by Caroline Woven

Poughkeepsie, NY

GET A GRIP

FOUND by Molly McGillicuddy

Stow, MA

to my valentine

I'll love you until the last one dies.

— Joey

Greetings...

...to the underwriter who is about to undertake evaluating the merits of refinancing my mortgage with your institution. You are charged with the responsibility of assessing the risk that will be assumed when you underwrite my refinancing plan. My goal is to help to minimize the risk. I have assembled the requested financial information to support my loan application. However, due to rather extenuating circumstances everything is not in the precise documentation you are accustomed to reviewing. I trust my explanations will allow you to waive some of your criteria.

As you review this material you will learn that I have filed three bankruptcies for the sole purpose of saving my home. The most important fact is that my third Chapter 13 plan filed in June of 1999 was successfully completed in July of 2004, and I would urge for an easement on the requirement for an applicant to have been out of bankruptcy for 2 years. My employment with Infinity Publishing made it possible for me to regain a firm financial footing. However, as I completed the plan – with every payment made on time – I was plunged into what would become pre-divorce turmoil that painfully drug on until the court approved divorce settlement, in September of 2005, that has caused me to seek refinancing to keep my home. My ex-wife will receive $57,000, the car, most of the furniture and household items as part of the divorce settlement. I get to refinance the house and to keep my constant companion Aurora – a stunning 6-year old Husky-Lab-Chow mix.

The ensuring bitterness and hatred from my ex-wife has made it impossible for me to provide some of the requested documentation. Her continuing harassment and abuse has thwarted my efforts to put my life back together again. My attorney filed a petition for a restraining order with the court after she trashed my office. Neither of us would leave the house because of the procession being nine tenths of the law factor and thusly I have endured the stressful strain of living under the same roof with her. With several occurrences of her recklessly endangering my life and Aurora's, I would have gladly moved out during this transition period. However, I had no where to temporarily move to and my home office is in my home. She has family in the area and I was most grateful for the times she stayed with them for a few days. I trust my substituted documentation will be sufficient for a favorable approval of my loan application. The loan proceeds would be used to pay my ex-wife the $57,000 as per the agreement, approximately $70,000 to pay off the balance of the mortgage held by Bruin Holdings – as per our agreement she has been making monthly payments to Bruin, and any additional proceeds being used for renovations and repairs to the house.

I am happy and secure in my position as Special Projects Director for **Eternal** Publishing. My boss, **Jed Parisons**, the company president, has been a most supportive colleague and friend during this horrific life transition. I trust that I will soon feel secure and happy with a new mortgage through your fine financial institution. In moving towards that successful conclusion, please read with due consideration being given to my explanations of rather extenuating situation, and if you have any questions regarding my employment **Mr. Parsons** can be reach at almost any time on his direct number (610) 473-3150, and any questions regarding the divorce settlement may be directed to my attorney, **Angie Tilson** at (215) 421-3147.

Thank you for the investment of your time and kind consideration of my application.

Paul D. Meadows

I subscribe to many of the beliefs of my ancestor, Ben Franklin, who said something like, "Know what you owe and pay what you owe." He also said, "The only two things that are certain in life are death and taxes."

EXPLANATION OF NO TAX RETURNS AND WORK HISTORY
Prepared by: **Paul D. Meadows** 11-11-05

The root of the problem is Bruin Holdings. After numerous requests for Bruin to provide 1098's, they provided only form letters stating that all the funds received via the bankruptcy court were applied, by their choice, to the interest on the loan. Therefore, they refused to provide the required 1098 forms. I urged the accountant to file and claim the money paid to Bruin as a deduction. The accountant refused by saying he could not knowingly do an incomplete filing. I consulted with a retired IRS agent and was told the proper way was to have the accountant attach the letters from Bruin with the filings and then let the IRS go after Bruin to produce the missing documentation. The accountant refused to pursue this recommended course of action, and therefore I refused to sign off on the filings.

From 1999 through 2004, while regular payments from my earnings were being made to the bankruptcy court to successfully complete the plan, a total of $94,508.09 was paid from my total earnings of $189,261.42 for the 5-year period under the protection of the bankruptcy plan. This means that I have a taxable annual income of approximately $18,500.00 to reconcile with the IRS. My monthly income is reflected on the included History of Earnings and as previously mentioned I will soon be a salaried employee. After the house is secure and the financial matters are sorted out I will be filing amended returns to resolve this issue.

I recently learned that in April of 1999, Bruin Holdings placed an additional $140,000 lien on the property at 11 Fountain Avenue, **Blakeland, CO-** this in addition to holding the paper on the property. The bankruptcy plan should have caused this lien to be removed by Bruin, however, it continues to be in force long after my bankruptcy plan was successfully completed in June 2004. The approximately $70,000 pay-off amount is the only monies owed to Bruin.

I trust due consideration will be given to my accrued credits for services rendered to the government and in community service. Beginning in my teens by serving as a cadet in the Civil Air Patrol (CAP), I served as the squadron's Information Service Officer (ISO) and as a Ranger-Certified member of a search and rescue team. The primary mission of the Civil Air Patrol was to provide domestic air search and rescue capabilities in support of USAF search operations. I learned to fly in the squadron's old L-16 aircraft.

In high school I was perhaps most noted for my involvement in extra-curricular actives of writing for the school newspaper with accompanying cartoons; participating in Youth-Day-In-Government by pressing for a third independent party being more representative of the student body rather two political parties composed of the student council and jocks. I was selected to be part of a student-teacher pilot program to interest high school students in a career as a teacher by teaching a sophomore art class. My academic achievements were at best slightly above average. My 1961 senior high school World Culture paper was "The German Problem" which addressed the divided Germany in the early '60's. The hardest grader in the school gave me an A++ with the notation that I blew getting a perfect A+++ with my summary foretelling of a reunited Germany. He told me in no uncertain terms that the world community would never allow a reunited Germany to happen in a million years. My logic back then was that the reunification would happen not from war or political deal doing, but rather from purely commercial needs to improve the regional economy.

After my graduation I enlisted in the USAF. While I was waiting to leave for basic training I learned I had been awarded a full 4-year scholarship to attend Millersville State Teachers College to become an art teacher. I called my recruiter to try to make a deal to serve in the USAF after college – not possible – I'd signed on the dotted-line and I was already in the service of my country. Previously I had the disappointing news from my pre-enlistment physical that my vision was off ever so slightly and I couldn't be an Air Force pilot. So I enlisted to serve as an Air Force illustrator – declining offers for flight training as a navigator or bombardier.

Most of my 4-year enlistment was spent as the Graphics Presentation Specialist for the 816th Strategic Aerospace Division, headquartered at Altus AFB, OK. I was responsible for the preparation of all briefing materials in addition to participating in evaluating Operational Readiness Inspections and going TDY on special duty assignments. One assignment had me "in country" in a country where we weren't in at the time. I designed the logo for the SAC PRIDE program – Professional Results In Daily Efforts. I earned 2-years of college credits under Operation Bootstrap and received an early-out by a few weeks in order to start my junior year of college at the beginning of the fall semester. My financial ability to complete college was made possible under the GI Bill and with a student loan which was repaid 2-years after graduation.

My free-lance commercial art business blossomed into an advertising design firm serving an impressive list of clients including Dodge Cork Company, Armstrong World Industries, RCA, Hamilton, Hilton, Cartech, and National Central Bank. In the mid '70's my interests evolved beyond the design firm to consulting on start-up operations and new product introductions. I loved the unique creative challenges that came with each assignment. After my successful self-publishing efforts in '72, my publishing credits increased thanks to my aggressive literary agent and my storytelling writing style.

I was very active in the Jaycees serving as President of the Lancaster chapter, editor-in-chief of the Colorado Jaycees monthly news magazine Future, and Special Assistant to the state president. I also served on the board of directors of Planned Parenthood of Lancaster County, the United Way, the American Heart Association, the Lancaster Advertising Club, and the Lancaster Chamber of Commerce.

In the early '80's my frustrations with the inaccuracies in market analysis statistics and other extenuating events plunged me into what would become almost 2-decades of doing primary research into the now popular area of pattern recognition analysis, however, my hypothesis was to prove the effectiveness of timeline data to support a stable forecast of future patterns. Basically my successful approach was combining aspects of fuzzy logic with the two-threshold concept of chaos theory. My methodology was flexible enough to identify when role-reversal occurred in a scored psychotherapy session; to measuring the potential for cross-over votes between Clinton, Bush and Perot; to accurately projecting tomorrow's closing price of traded stocks. Research grants came from several members of the financial community interested in developing technical-trading applications for forecasting movements in the stocks and bonds market.

During this research and development period I found the need to balance my right/left brain activity. My logical formulating efforts by day were transformed into doing creative fun writings by night. Some of my writings made it onto the web via several ezines, which resulted in readers requesting that I publish a collection of my work. In the late '90's my search for a publisher lead me to Eternal Publishing. Soon after they published ENJOY OFTEN!!! in March of 1999, Jed Parsons offered me a position as their first Author's Advocate with the responsibility of developing the program that introduces authors to Eternal's unique way of publishing. In my current position as Special Projects Director I am responsible for overseeing the activity of our 3 Author's Advocates as well as editing our monthly Author's Advocate Newsletter. I'm responsible for our annual "Express Yourself..." Authors' Conference and I also direct several special seminar presentations each year in various parts of the country. I represent Eternal Publishing as an invited presenter at publishing seminars, conferences, and industry summits.

A retiring vice-president with National Central Bank once told me that when he was a young loan officer at a rural branch office, a farmer came in to apply for a divorce loan to pay for the lawyering and court costs. My friend explained they didn't have a divorce loan, just new car and home improvement loans. The farmer asked to be fixed him up with one of them home improvement loans because being rid of her would be a major home improvement. Indeed I am also involved in a major home improvement project and I need your favorable loan approval to secure my home and to keep the improvements happening in a timely fashion.

Due to the hostile domestic situation and bitter divorce that has dragged on for over 2-years, I lack some of the requested supporting documentation regarding my earnings and tax returns. I understand that there is normally a 2-year period for a person to be out of bankruptcy before consideration is given for them to be worthy of approval for a loan. However, I trust your kind consideration will given to the above with regards to my ability to make positive things happen, my public service, and the fact that my use of the bankruptcy law was to save my home and to avoid defaulting on the loan. Please note, the only items included in the bankruptcy were the house and taxes Bruin Holdings failed to pay. Naturally I would urge for prompt approval as I am most eager to successfully resolve these financial issues as soon as possible.

Thank you for your time and due consideration.

Sincerely,

Paul D. Meadows

FAX NO.   4122060051   P. 12
P.06

MAY-19-2006 FRI 09:33 AM   AB CAPITAL   MAY 16,2006
MAY-16-2006 15:30

Derogatory Items:

To Whom IT May Concern:

There are no words or explanations that I can explain for my past delinquencies but I will try. The last two years has very trying on me with deaths and hard ships that spilled over to my finance life but everyone has a sad story to tell.

Hopefully, this sad story will end with the approval of this loan and I can square up with my past latencies.

I can assure you that this credit issue will be resolve and the majority of debit will be paid off if loan is approved.

Best Regards,

Walters

STARZ

FOUND by Brian Frye

Boston, MA

I was taking out the trash at work and discovered this depressing reminder of how disconnected and lonely people are. I think that is common.

-B.F.

Dr. Henderson,

As I said my first hospitalization at 19 was catastrophic. I held on until I was 23 when I found out through the Grapevine about Starzy on the other side of town in an Industrial Park in the back of a factory it was a Disco with all the trimmings if I scored a name and number I went home in anticipation of friendship first. If not I went trolling for leftovers like me. When I made a friend I couldn't have sex with them. I had a good sense of humor but it wasn't enough. When I did have sex it fell apart quickly. I think that is common.

Illustration by Carson Mell

82

foundmagazine.com

this photo FOUND by Natalia Korshin, Anchorage, AK

Get bit by Bitner!

YOUR FINDS ARE OUR JOB #1!

foundmagazine.com's Jason Bitner discusses the art of the perfect find.

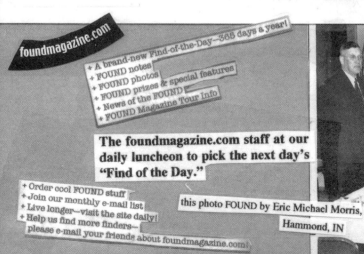

foundmagazine.com

+ A brand-new Find-of-the-Day—365 days a year!
+ FOUND notes
+ FOUND photos
+ FOUND prizes & special features
+ News of the FOUND
+ FOUND Magazine Tour Info

The foundmagazine.com staff at our daily luncheon to pick the next day's "Find of the Day."

+ Order cool FOUND stuff
+ Join our monthly e-mail list
+ Live longer—visit the site daily!
+ Help us find more finders—please e-mail your friends about foundmagazine.com!

this photo FOUND by Eric Michael Morris, Hammond, IN

OUR FOUND MAGAZINE

SPONSORS

ARE TONALLY AWWWSUMMM!!!

All the amazing folks on the following pages have made it possible for us to print the magazine you're holding in your hands! We adore our sponsors and deeply appreciate their support—and we hope you'll support them by checking out their wonderful services, products, and projects. Thanks a million!!

YOU DOTH PROTEST TOO MUCH
FOUND by Jordan Stolte and Carey Chesney
Ann Arbor, MI

YOU'RE ALL "IM FROM THE MIDWEST. IM NOT A SLUT. IM FROM THE MIDWEST. I DON'T GIVE BLOW-JOBS!"

back   front

HEY DAVY !
THANKS FOR
LETTING US
ANIMATE ⌐ **FOUND**

YOUR FANS 4-EVER ➜

seesaw studios
www.seesawstudios.com

The River City Roller Girls are an all female roller derby league in Richmond Virginia

OUR season goes all year long! Check the web for current schedules!

RCR WANTS YOU!
We recruit women 18+ to skate, & male/female support staff all year round.
No experience needed!

Contact us for more details! See you on the track!

www.myspace.com/rivercityrollergirls
www.rivercityrollergirls.org

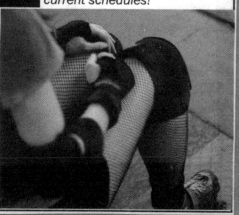

VAULT OF MIDNIGHT

219 S. MAIN ST.
ANN ARBOR, MI 48104

MON-SAT: 10-10
SUNDAYS: 11-8

www.VAULTOFMIDNIGHT.com
734-998-1413

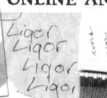

SAGUARO
The Life & Adventures of Bobby Allen Bird
A novel by Carson Mell

"Bobby Bird is one of the most tragic, funny and indelible characters I've ever discovered in a book -- and I've read a lot of books. *Saguaro* is in the top ten."

--Davy Rothbart

AVAILABLE AT WWW.CARSONMELL.COM

THE END OF SOCIETY BY THE YEAR 2012. STAY TUNED

THE END
FOUND by Dennis Morley   in downtown Los Angeles, CA

FOOTPRINTS ON OUR HEARTS
Jamaica Plains, MA
FOUND by Anna Koon

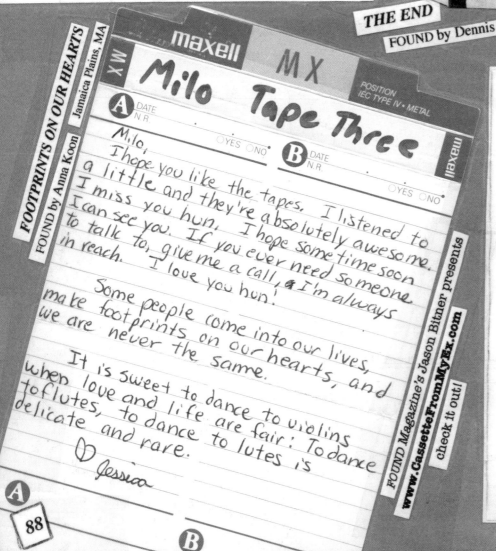

maxell XW MX
Milo Tape Three
POSITION IEC TYPE IV · METAL

(A) DATE N.R.   ○YES ○NO   (B) DATE N.R.   ○YES ○NO

Milo,
I hope you like the tapes. I listened to a little and they're absolutely awesome. I miss you hun. I hope sometime soon I can see you. If you ever need someone to talk to, give me a call, & I'm always in reach. I love you hun!

Some people come into our lives, make footprints on our hearts, and we are never the same.

It is sweet to dance to violins when love and life are fair; To dance to flutes, to dance to lutes is delicate and rare.

♡
Jessica

(A)
88
(B)

SUICIDEGIRLS.com
❤ redefine beauty ✶

Dear female readers,
get NAKED and get paid!
apply now at suicidegirls.com

From: models@suicidegirls.com
Subject: **RE: I WANT TO GET NAKED FOR SUICIDEGIRLS!!!!**
Date: March 20, 2007 3:21:19 PM PST
To: ~~████████████████████~~

1. Apply! Go to *www.suicidegirls.com/model* and fill in the form. The pics you include should show you clearly and to your best advantage. Try to let your personality come through.

2. We'll reply to you! Once weve received your application, well get back to you and let you know if we need any more info. Once we have everything we need, youll get a login and password to our special model applicants section.

3. Send in your set. When youve received your login and password, youll see everything we need from you to get you set up as a SuicideGirl. Follow the steps and youre on your way!

Must I be 18 or older?
Yes. Please make sure your local laws allow you to pose nude before applying. Usually you must be 18 years of age or older to apply. If you are in Alabama you must be 19 or older. If you are in Mississippi, Nebraska, Pennsylvania, or Puerto Rico you must be 21 or older.

Do you pay for photos?
Yes! We pay $500 for e ach photoset that we accept.

Can you hook me up with a photographer?
Probably! We have official photographers all over the world. Contact our Model Coordinator who can help you locate an official SG photographer near you.

Do I have to be a skinny white girl?
No. We enourage women of all body types and skin colours to apply. If you are confident and sexy, we want to hear from you! (It's okay if you are a skinny white girl. We love you too.)

QUACK!MEDIA + LETTERFORM

VARIOUS PUBLISHING BASED IN ANN ARBOR, MI + SMALLISH GRAPHIC DESIGN OUT OF CHICAGO, IL

A HEALTHY PAIR CREATING THOUGHTFUL WORK SINCE 2006.

QUACKMEDIA.COM + LETTERFORM.NET

FOUND MAGAZINE'S LIVE TOUR!!

FALL 2008 * EUROPE

SPRING 2009 * UNITED STATES

Davy & Peter Rothbart present a smash-'em-up good time for all! Find out when *FOUND* will be in your city at www.foundmagazine.com and www.21balloons.com

Hey! Did you know there's a FOUND *book*?! Actually, there's *two* of 'em! Each one's got a few favorite finds from the mags, plus 212 pages of all-new finds. Pick 'em up at *any* bookstore, or order online at amazon.com or foundmagazine.com. Dang.

"A fascinating and wonderfully moving collage of human emotion."
—Jessica Hundley, *Los Angeles Times*

'FOUND'
THE BEST LOST, TOSSED, AND FORGOTTEN ITEMS FROM AROUND THE WORLD

THE NATIONAL BESTSELLER

DAVY ROTHBART
CREATOR OF FOUND MAGAZINE

Available wherever books are sold.

Dear Friends...

aminibigcircus.com

'FOUND' II

DAVY ROTHBART
Author of the National Bestseller FOUND

MORE OF THE BEST LOST, TOSSED, AND FORGOTTEN ITEMS FROM AROUND THE WORLD

POLAROIDS

FOUND by Katie Lacy, East Lansing, MI; Amy Trowbridge-Yates, Kansas City, MO; E.T., Seattle, WA; Isaac Nichols, Philadelphia, PA; Molly, Akron, OH; Kelly Richardson, Bloomington, IN; Ralph Spight, San Francisco, CA; Kibble Smith, New York City, NY

HEY! CHECK OUT OUR...

FOUND
POLAROIDS
BOOK!!!

'FOUND'

POLAROIDS

® POLAROID ® POLAROID ® POLAROID ® POLAROID ® POLAROID ®

"Polaroid film is expensive but that doesn't stop people from forgetting their pictures all over the place. Lucky for all of us, FOUND has been collecting the ones left behind for years, keeping a formidable stash of the blurry, the mysterious, the touching and the unexplainable..."

—Venus Zine

FOUND

SEND THIS ORDER TO

Name	
Address	

City	State	Zip	Country

Email	
Phone	

☐ **This is a gift! Please fill out the below information in case FOUND has any questions about your order**

Name	Phone	Email

All listed prices are for U.S. orders. For international orders, double the shipping price for each item.

QUANTITY	PUBLICATIONS		ITEM PRICE	TOTAL
	The First Four	The first four issues of FOUND for one price	$25	
	FOUND Issue #1	Kicked it all off.	$8 ($5 + $3 shipping)	
	FOUND Issue #2	112 pages of FOUND!	$8 ($5 + $3 shipping)	
	FOUND Issue #3	It's all about love.	$8 ($5 + $3 shipping)	
	FOUND Issue #4	Come into our world.	$8 ($5 + $3 shipping)	
	FOUND Issue #5	The Crime Issue.	$8 ($5 + $3 shipping)	
	DIRTY FOUND #1	2 hardcore 4 FOUND Magazine *Must be 18+ to order*	$13 ($10 + $3 shipping)	
	DIRTY FOUND #2	2 hardcore 4 FOUND Magazine *Must be 18+ to order*	$13 ($10 + $3 shipping)	
	DIRTY FOUND #3	2 hardcore 4 FOUND Magazine *Must be 18+ to order*	$13 ($10 + $3 shipping)	
	FOUND Polaroid Book	A full-color limited-edition art book of the world's best FOUND Polaroids	$29 ($25 + $4 shipping)	
	FOUND Issue #6	IN MY LIFE	$8 ($5+$3 shipping)	

OTHER SHWAG

QUANTITY	PUBLICATIONS		ITEM PRICE	TOTAL
	FOUND Greeting Cards	Greet in style; set of 12	$27 ($24 + $3 shipping)	
	T Shirt	Pick your size: XS, S, M, L, XL	$15 ($12 + $3 shipping)	
	Booty CD	21 booty-thumpin' tracks. "The Booty Don't Stop!"	$12 ($9 + $3 shipping)	
	7" Vinyl Single	4 FOUND-inspired songs by Jon Langford, TRS-80, Claudine Coule, and The Victrolas	$7 ($5 + $2 shipping)	
	Bumper Sticker		$1.50 ($1 + .50 shipping)	
	1" Button		$1.50 ($1 + .50 shipping)	

send to:

**Quack! Media
320 S. Main St., A
Ann Arbor, MI 48104**

Allow 4-6 weeks for delivery
Questions? contact us at info@quackmedia.com
Order FOUND online at www.foundmagazine.com

TOTAL PRICE $

PAYMENT METHOD

☐ Well-concealed cash

☐ Money order

☐ Check
make payable to
Quack! Media

Who has
That dirt wheels

Mag — It's not
Dirt wheels, it's
dirt rider, I saw the June Dirt wheel,
It has a few good articles, one about Twist throttle
vs thumb throttle.

ROUGH RIDERS ROLL

FOUND by Stephen Altobello   Brooklyn, NY

7" VINYL
$3

FOUND MAGAZINE ISSUES $5 each

FOUND
magazine

FOUND BUMPER STICKER: $1

FOUND BUTTON: $1   "THE BOOTY DON'T STOP" CD $10

95

THANKS FOR SENDING IN YOUR FINDS!

this photo was FOUND near the Solid Waste Transfer Station
by Gordon Maurer, Kirkland, WA

OUR MAILBOX IS ALWAYS OPEN!

FOUND Magazine
3455 Charing Cross Road
Ann Arbor, MI
48108-1911

Questions? contact us at info@foundmagazine.com

96